Interpretive
Discussion

Interpretive Discussion

ENGAGING STUDENTS IN TEXT-BASED CONVERSATIONS

Sophie Haroutunian-Gordon

HARVARD EDUCATION PRESS

Cambridge, Massachusetts

Library of Congress Control Number 2013951060

Paperback ISBN 978-1-61250-644-9
Library Edition ISBN 978-1-61250-645-6

Published by Harvard Education Press,
an imprint of the Harvard Education Publishing Group

Harvard Education Press
8 Story Street
Cambridge, MA 02138

Cover Design: Deborah Hodgdon
Cover Photo: Frederic Cirou/PhotoAlto/Corbis

The typefaces used in this book are Adobe Caslon Pro and Avenir.

Contents

For Obi, Iké, and Ijé,
three beautiful grandsons

Fruitful analysis is the result of spontaneous reaction
to some musical detail that puzzles the musician so that he
investigates what happens here in particular.

—Konrad Wolff, paraphrasing pianist Arthur Schnabel,
The Teaching of Arthur Schnabel: A Guide to Interpretation

Interpretation of any discussable text
begins with a puzzle.

Foreword

I AM DELIGHTED to write this foreword, not only because Sophie Haroutunian-Gordon has been a friend and colleague for more than forty years, but also because I believe deeply in the educative value of interpretive discussion for all students, especially in a democratic society. I also believe that teachers at every level and stage of their career can enrich and strengthen their teaching by learning the discussion-leading patterns and practices presented in this book. Participating in interpretive discussions can help teachers and students alike learn to use their minds with power and pleasure.

Haroutunian-Gordon introduced me to the concept of interpretive discussion when we worked together in the Master of Science in Teaching Program at the University of Chicago in the 1970s. Inspired by the Junior Great Books approach to discussion that she encountered as a sixth-grade teacher, she taught our elementary teacher candidates how to prepare for and lead interpretive discussions of children's literature. Students prepared clusters of questions and practiced leading discussions first with their peers and then with small groups of children in their practicum sites. The teachers also tape-recorded these discussions in order to study their practice and its impact on students' thinking and participation.

Over a long and fruitful career, Haroutunian-Gordon has explored the philosophy and practice of interpretive discussion through a dynamic program of scholarship and teacher education. She has conceptualized the intellectual foundations of interpretive discussion, elaborated its distinctive pedagogy, studied its patterns and impact on teachers and students, and designed unique systems for inducting others into this powerful educational practice. At the annual reunions of the American Educational Research Association, I listened with admiration and interest as she described how she transformed her philosophy of education course in the Master of Science in Education Program at Northwestern University into an interpretive-discussion laboratory. Elementary and secondary teacher candidates experienced the intellectual challenges and satisfaction of interpretive discussion as they searched for meaning in the required texts of the course (Dewey, Plato, Rousseau); teaching assistants, mainly doctoral students and alumni of the program, learned to prepare for and lead such discussions under Haroutunian-Gordon's guidance. Through this unique experience, scores of aspiring and practicing teachers were introduced to the power and practice of interpretive discussion that they, in turn, introduced to their students.

Three important books grew out of this work: *Turning the Soul: Teaching Through Conversation in the High School* (1991), *Learning to Teach Through Discussion: The Art of Turning the Soul* (2009), and now the present volume, *Interpretive Discussion: Engaging Students in Text-Based Conversations* (2014). This book offers a valuable guide to the intellectual and practical work of interpretive discussion. As Haroutunian-Gordon promises in her introduction, the book aims to "help educators practice the rewarding art of interpretive discussion with success and satisfaction."

Haroutunian-Gordon takes us inside her thinking as she prepares for, leads (or coleads), and reflects on three interpretive discussions. In following her extensive examples and close-up analysis, we get a grounded understanding of each phase of the work, from selecting a discussable text and framing a set of questions, to asking for textual evidence and determining the strength of an argument, to reflecting on whether the discussion has surfaced a "shared point of doubt" and whether participants have made progress toward resolving it. We also learn about the complexities and uncertainties of the work. It is humbling to realize that even a skilled discussion leader like Haroutunian-Gordon puzzles about what speakers mean and whether she made the right move to help clarify a student's thinking. It is inspiring to see how interpretive discussion helps teachers and students alike get better at questioning and listening.

Haroutunian-Gordon has produced a powerful tool for serious and sustained teacher development, focused on a core practice that belongs in the repertoire of all teachers. In the opening chapter, she suggests that interpretive discussion is one way to achieve the analytic skills and understanding called for in the Common Core Standards. "Leading discussions" also appears in contemporary lists of high-leverage teaching practices, core practices that provide a basis for responsible, independent teaching (see www.teachingworks.org).

This book can help teachers develop a shared vision and understanding of interpretive discussion and its flexible uses across subjects and grade levels. The framework, annotated examples, and appendixes can structure and guide teachers' joint work as they prepare questions, colead discussions, observe and analyze classroom experiments, and discuss emergent questions and problems. As teachers gain confidence and skill through collaborative experimentation and development, they can also study the impact of participating in such discussions on students' confidence and academic skills. In short, Haroutunian-Gordon's book offers a curriculum for teacher learning at every career stage.

Reading this book, you will find it hard to defend the view that good teachers are born, not made. Haroutunian-Gordon provides compelling evidence that a core teaching practice like leading interpretive discussions can be taught and learned by teachers, but not without serious and sustained effort. And what better way to strengthen the quality of teaching and learning in our schools?

I hope that this book will become a primer for teachers, teacher educators, and professional developers, helping teachers across the country to learn, teach, and practice the art of interpretive discussion.

Sharon Feiman-Nemser
Mandel Professor of Jewish Education
Brandeis University

Introduction

I really want students to understand that they can come up with interpretations of a text without a teacher telling them what it's actually about, so that they [can] engage in meaningful discussion.

—Lindsay, *English teacher at an urban high school*

THE GOAL OF helping students to think for themselves about the meaning of objects that they encounter, whether these be books, sets of data, films, musical compositions, paintings—indeed, any object whose meaning is unclear—is not new. Yet, in many classrooms and informal learning situations, the goal remains elusive. In 1980, Jean Anyon wrote that the goal itself was absent in classrooms that she observed serving low-achieving students.[1]

Times have changed in the following sense: today, more than forty-five states in America have adopted the Common Core State Standards, which require that all students in grades K–12 learn to interpret texts. For example, College and Career Readiness Anchor Standards for those in grades K–5 state that students should be able to "read closely to determine what the text says explicitly and make logical inferences from it; cite specific textual evidence when writing or speaking to support conclusions drawn from the text."

The standard insists that students be able to comprehend what is stated explicitly in a text, infer what follows logically from the explicit statement, and make

1

arguments based on textual evidence to support those inferences, or interpret a text for themselves.

Furthermore, students in grades 3–5 should be able to "engage effectively in a range of collaborative discussions with diverse partners on grade level topics and texts, building on others' ideas and expressing their own clearly."

Thus, students should also be able to engage in conversation about the meaning of texts with others, whose perspectives and backgrounds may differ from their own. The exchanges will be "collaborative," meaning that students will work together to develop ideas—"building on others' ideas"—and state their views clearly.

How are these goals of the Common Core State Standards to be realized, considering that in many school settings, they have proved elusive? In the pages that follow, I present one approach to teaching and learning that may be helpful, what I call *interpretive discussion*. The approach helps students and teachers acquire knowledge and analytic skills, including those of questioning, argument construction and evaluation, and refined speaking and listening ability. It asks students and teachers to question the meaning of what they see and hear, so that they can better understand what they encounter.

Participation in interpretive discussion does more. It helps people form cooperative communities that work together to identify and pursue the resolution of shared questions and concerns. We will discover the strength of such communities throughout this book.

The present volume is, in fact, the third book that I have written about interpretive discussion. The first, *Turning the Soul: Teaching Through Conversation in the High School*, presents it as a powerful pedagogy grounded in a vision of education that grows out of Plato, Rousseau, and Dewey.[2] In *Turning the Soul*, two high school groups—one group composed of experienced discussants in an urban private school called Chalmers, and the second composed of special-education students in an urban public school called Belden—discuss the meaning of Shakespeare's *Romeo and Juliet*. While initially, the students at Chalmers spin interpretations of the characters with the ease of a disk jockey and those at Belden stare speechless before Shakespeare's text, the two groups come to look more and more alike as their experience with interpretative discussion proceeds. Indeed, students in both schools seem to learn that they do have ideas about the nature of the characters and

Shakespeare's meaning, yet defending those ideas requires careful interpretation of the text and argument formation.

The second book, *Learning to Teach Through Discussion: The Art of Turning the Soul*, is a research study of two teacher education candidates at Northwestern University who were learning to lead interpretive discussion. There, I elaborate on how the conceptual foundations of the pedagogy include visions of questioning (e.g., Gadamer, Jauss), of discourse theory (e.g., Bakhtin, Grice), of theories of reading (e.g., Iser, Donoghue, Rosenblatt), of learning as explored through learning sciences (e.g., Pea, Edelson and Reiser, Resnick, Schoenfeld), and of psychological theory (e.g. Lave, Lave and Wenger).[3]

The book that you hold in your hands is different kind of book. It is meant to be a resource—a tool that can help readers develop the knowledge, skills, values, and habits of mind that are required for the successful use of interpretive discussion as a pedagogical orientation. The book rests on the conceptual foundations and research presented in the earlier volumes. Here, I ground the analysis not only in the aforementioned traditions but also in my experiences as an elementary and secondary student at the Francis W. Parker School in Chicago, a sixth-grade teacher (Glencoe, Illinois), my training as a philosopher of education (University of Chicago), a pianist, and my life as a philosopher and teacher educator in the School of Education and Social Policy at Northwestern University, where I directed the Master of Science in Education Program for twenty-two years.

As I have argued elsewhere, interpretive discussion is a set of practices that enable both students and teachers to focus on rather than ignore what they do not understand, and to address points of doubt about the meaning of objects by questioning, scrutinizing, speaking, listening, and reasoning.[4] Every interpretive discussion is unique, and the experiences of preparing for, participating in, and leading these discussions are always novel. As a consequence, it is not possible to provide lockstep, cookbook-like procedures for success.

On the contrary, I hope to provide, first of all, a series of illustrations that will help readers develop insight into the three phases of interpretive discussion—preparation, leading, and reflection. In addition, I hope the book will offer both inspiration and direction in cultivating the values, skills, and habits of mind needed to engage in the three phases. Hence, it should help educators to practice the rewarding art of interpretive discussion with success and satisfaction. The understanding, skills, and habits of mind that I describe in these chapters have proven efficacious. The aim of this book is to help you cultivate these advantages and to embrace opportunities for so doing by recognizing the possibilities for effective response.

Of course, interpretive discussion is not the only thing to do with students in the classroom. Lecture, demonstration, and, indeed, many traditional school learning activities may be appropriate at moments, even more appropriate than interpretive discussion. Yet, traditional school experiences often fail to ask students to think for themselves—to identify questions they wish to resolve and to find evidence that addresses the questions. Traditionally, students in classrooms—even college classrooms—are not asked to interpret evidence and to use their interpretations to address their questions. That is, they are not encouraged to raise questions and build convincing arguments in support of their resolutions. Interpretive discussion and related activities provide opportunities to do these things. Often, pursuit of the activities helps cooperative groups to form.

The remainder of the introduction is divided into three sections. The first defines the term *interpretive discussion*. The second summarizes the benefits that can accrue to both students and teachers who engage in interpretive discussion—benefits that I have discovered through research and professional experience. The third section presents an overview of the book.

WHAT IS INTERPRETIVE DISCUSSION?

Interpretive discussion aims to develop and address questions about the meaning of texts, rather than simply extracting information from them or judging their worth.[5] Does it sound familiar? Perhaps you participated in interpretive discussion as part of your own school experience without ever having heard the term. If you did, you may remember sitting in a circle with twelve to fifteen other students and your teacher or possibly another leader or pair of coleaders. You may have read the text under discussion before coming together with others, or the leader may have read it to you.

During an interpretive discussion, the group works together to identify a question about the meaning of the text. The question may be about a character's motivation, the author's beliefs, or the meaning of a term as it is used in the text, for example. The question is a genuine question—one to which not even the leader is sure of the answer. As the question concerning the group becomes clear, the members work to resolve it by studying different parts of the text that seem to have implication for its resolution.

Interpretive discussion might be thought of as suitable only for "elite" schools, where students know how to read and reflect.[6] Many elementary school communities offer Junior Great Books discussions as an extracurricular activity, and of all the popular discussion approaches, interpretive discussion is most closely akin to the one suggested by Junior Great Books.[7] However, interpretive discussion should not be relegated to afterschool or lunchtime activities; it is useful not just for strong readers experienced in text interpretation. And it is suitable not just for the study of literature.

On the contrary, interpretive discussion helps all students develop resources that are critical to successful reading, to academic study in many disciplines, and to success in a democratic society.[8] Consequently, it should play a fundamental role in a student's school experience, regardless of grade level, subject focus, or academic giftedness. Interpretive discussion is not an alternative to lecture and direct teaching, or even other kinds of discussion. But it develops academic and social-emotional resources that many of these other modes of instruction neglect.

SOME BENEFITS OF INTERPRETIVE DISCUSSION

Let me mention some benefits that can accrue to students who participate in interpretive discussion.

First, as we will see, it teaches them to work together to identify questions they wish to resolve. Identifying clear questions is generally neglected in lecture or didactic instruction, whose aim is to impart information or skills. Indeed, cultivating clear questions is frequently ignored by discussion approaches that seek to encourage expression of feelings or to arrive at interpretations of texts that teachers take to be correct.[9] By contrast, interpretive discussion helps discussants clarify their questions—the things they do not understand and wish to find out. In so doing, they learn to question the meaning of what has been said—by the text, by others, and by themselves. Furthermore, they learn to identify and ponder evidence in the text to support their ideas about meaning. Through that conversation, they identify a question that they and others in the group care to resolve—what I call the *shared point of doubt*.

Second, interpretive discussion helps people learn to listen. The listening that it cultivates is not a passive reception of information, as is required when you listen to a lecture. Nor is it listening so as to follow instruction, as direct teaching demands. And it is not simply polite listening that waits its turn. Rather, it is listening so as to grasp intended meaning—listening that itself involves questioning and relating ideas to one another so as to identify an intention that may well be implicit.[10]

Third, interpretive discussion helps participants form and evaluate the soundness of arguments in the service of seeking to understand. Once the group has come to a shared point of doubt, members try to identify textual evidence that addresses the point and helps resolve it. Argument construction and evaluation is an explicit focus of an interpretive discussion.

Fourth, because interpretive discussion develops skills and habits of mind that enable questioning and listening, it helps participants to form cooperative groups to achieve shared goals—goals of their own making. Working together as they do, members come to care about one another as thinking, resourceful beings whose contributions are sought after.[11]

The benefits of interpretive discussion accrue to leaders as well as discussants. For example, before engaging the participants in the conversation, leaders have identified a question about the meaning of the text to be discussed. This is a question about which they have curiosity—a question that they wish to resolve for its own sake. Arriving at such a question puts leaders in the role of seeker—one who does not know and who is trying to find out. They come to the discussion ready to listen to the participants to gain a clearer understanding of the text themselves.

In becoming a seeker, leaders resolve many things about what the text does mean, and thus, they become very familiar with it. Hence, they can help a group clarify its questions and locate passages relevant to its concerns, even if these are not related to questions they cultivated prior to the discussion.

Furthermore, because leaders come to the discussion familiar with the text yet desirous of further understanding, they develop leading and listening patterns that help them and the participants to question more fully what is said. In my research, I have identified some of the more successful leading patterns.[12] In the chapters that follow, we see the how following these patterns helps both leaders and discussants to question and listen better, that is, to understand intended meaning more clearly. Some leading patterns are carried out with the specific purpose of helping speakers express themselves more precisely and thus helping others understand their intended meaning more fully.

So why do leading and participating in interpretive discussion help people acquire skills and habits of mind that are needed for active citizenship in a democratic society?[13] The fact is, participants and leaders bring diverse perspectives to the text. The perspectives may vary with the age, gender, personal history, cultural heritage, socioeconomic status, physical health, and personal interests, for example. In leading and participating in interpretive discussion, the leader and discussants, like citizens in a democratic society, must learn to do the following:

- Question one another about the meaning of the text,—the sets of issues and facts before them—to clarify the point of doubt that they will work together to resolve.
- Listen to grasp speakers' intended meanings, which requires tolerance.[14] This kind of tolerance allows people who have different perspectives to work together to grasp and hear the concerns of one another and to identify questions of shared concern.[15]
- Work together to develop solutions to the issues they wish to resolve. Together, they need to be able to find, interpret, and evaluate evidence relevant to a sound resolution.

By leading and participating in interpretive discussions, people learn the skills and habits of mind necessary for all three of these activities.

OVERVIEW OF THE BOOK

The overall purpose of the book is to help teachers become effective leaders of interpretive discussion and thus develop the resources needed to successfully engage in its three phases: preparation, leading, and reflection. The book is divided into three parts, seven chapters, and a conclusion. Also included are six appendixes that may be distributed to leaders and participants. These summarize suggested procedures for preparing, leading, participating in, and reflecting upon interpretive discussions.

Chapter 1 presents a detailed overview of the three phases of interpretive discussion—preparation, leading, and reflection—so that the reader may begin to grasp what each phase involves. In the same chapter, I introduce the first of three discussions that are considered at length in subsequent chapters—a discussion of *Schoolmaster*, a poem by Yevgeny Yevtushenko.[16] The discussion took place between a group of high school sophomores and me as the leader.

Part 1, "Preparation," includes two chapters. Chapter 2 describes the initial task of preparing to lead an interpretive discussion—that of selecting a text. Here, I explain more fully what I mean by the term *text*. A text suitable for interpretive discussion is one in which the leader finds ambiguity. Questioning enables the leader to clarify a point of ambiguity and, in so doing, come to care about resolving it.

Also in chapter 2, I introduce two more texts whose discussion by students will be detailed in later chapters. The first text, discussed by students in a seventh-grade science class, is "Rats," an excerpt from a work by the ethologist Konrad Lorenz. The second text, the Nobel Laureate speech delivered by Toni Morrison in 1993, was discussed by a group of high school seniors. In chapter 2, I question the Yevtushenko poem as well as these additional texts to develop a point of doubt that I have about their meaning.

Chapter 3 presents the second task of preparation, namely, developing what I call a *cluster of questions*. Not every point of ambiguity that you identify in studying a text can sustain or is worthy of a forty-five-minute discussion. To determine whether a point of doubt is worthy, leaders can develop a set of interpretive questions that address it. The cluster consists of a basic question, which expresses the point of ambiguity, and eight follow-up questions. Each of these questions points to a passage in the text which, if interpreted in at least one way, suggests an idea about resolving the basic question. Each question in the cluster is interpretive, meaning that it may be answered in more than one way, in light of textual evidence. In chapter 3, we see how a cluster of questions about *Schoolmaster* grew out of an ambiguity that arose as I wrote questions about the text.

Part 2, "Leading the Discussion," includes three chapters, each of which presents excerpts from an interpretive discussion that actually took place. We see the leader following discussion-leading patterns. The students respond—to the leader, the text, and to one another. While the leader begins by initiating certain patterns, the discussants begin to do likewise as the conversations continue. We see evidence of the discussants' learning to do things that help them interpret texts. And in each case, the group moves toward the twofold goal of an interpretive discussion, coming to a question that participants share about the meaning of the text and making progress toward resolution. We also see cooperative working groups beginning to form.

Chapter 4 presents excerpts from the discussion of *Schoolmaster*, which took place at a suburban private school that I call Aurora.[17] After an initial exchange between the leader and one participant, other discussants enter the discussion, and a shared point of doubt begins to arise. The participants move toward more careful attempts to interpret passages fully and build arguments for their interpretations. They listen to one another—working to grasp what others intend to say and hence treating them as valued contributors.

Chapter 5 offers excerpts from the discussion of "Rats," which took place at a middle school with an ethnically diverse population located near an urban area. The discussants were seventh-grade science students at a school called Pine Grove, and their teacher, Ms. Prentice, prepared for and co-led the discussion with me. The group discussed the text fishbowl style—half the group watching while the other half conversed and reversing roles halfway through the discussion. Those in the first group seemed to open a question about the meaning of the text—a question that those in the second group continued to address.

Chapter 6 analyzes excerpts from the discussion of Toni Morrison's Nobel Laureate lecture. The discussants were a group of racially and ethnically diverse high school seniors who attended a "low-performing" school that I call Canterbury. Like those in the seventh-grade science class, these students were inexperienced with interpretive discussion. Yet, also like that group, they come to a shared point of doubt. The discussants make clear progress addressing their question by following and initiating patterns that enable them to identify and interpret relevant textual evidence. They help each other develop convincing arguments by initiating and responding to effective discussion-leading patterns.

Part 3, "Reflection," includes two chapters. In chapter 7, we reflect on the three discussions considered in chapters 4, 5, and 6 and ask, If a shared point of doubt did arise in the group, how did it arise from what was said? And was progress made toward resolution? In addressing these questions, we also reflect on what happened to the group as it pursued its goals and to the individuals who participated in the conversation. Finally, we consider the impact that the cluster of questions, formed by the leader or leaders before each discussion, had on the course of each conversation.

In the book's conclusion, various teachers describe their experiences with interpretive discussion in their classrooms. The teachers reflect on the use of the approach at a variety of grade levels, including elementary, middle, and high school, and with a variety of subject matters, such as English language arts, mathematics, science, and world language. Some of the teachers have found interpretive discussion to be challenging. Many, like Jason, an eighth-grade language arts teacher, have found it powerful and provocative:

> **JASON:** I run professional development in my school. We are working to help teachers integrate interpretive discussion along with dialectical journaling throughout their reading curriculum.
>
> A lot of the students are pigeonholed as those that couldn't handle interpretive discussion. Yet, they are the ones that in many respects can handle it the best. What I mean by that is a student might struggle with language processing—might really have a hard time decoding the text. But many of these kids are the ones that have such fantastic ideas and that really love the discussion process. I've seen it happen so many times: a student who is perhaps a low reader is really an insightful student. The problem is not the lack of insight but functional literacy. And I think that if you can work with those populations, you can get kids really excited.
>
> One teacher I have spoken with about this is the special-education reading teacher in my grade, eighth grade. She's a phenomenally talented teacher who does incredible things with her students. Now, her students might struggle discerning what the text says, but when it comes to talking about what's going on in the book, they're fantastic. So one step I'd like to take is teaming up with this special-ed teacher. If we could both accomplish it with both classes, I think that would be so powerful.[18]

Jason seems excited about the potential of interpretive discussion to engage students in dialogue about the meaning of texts, even students with limited reading proficiency. In the conclusion, we will hear more from Jason and other teachers who are realizing that potential.

Let us now begin our exploration of the interpretive discussion pedagogy.

The Three Phases of Interpretive Discussion

As EXPLAINED IN the introduction, interpretive discussion is discussion about the meaning of some text. The text may be a book, a painting, a film, a piece of recorded music, a musical score, a set of data—indeed, any object whose meaning is ambiguous. The purpose of the discussion is to make progress in understanding the text. The progress is made by a group of discussants—often ten to fifteen—and a leader or pair of coleaders. The group tries to come to a shared point of doubt about the meaning of the text—a question that most if not all wish to resolve—and to address it by studying the evidence presented in the text.

Interpretive discussion, a pedagogical orientation toward the study of meaning, has three phases. This chapter presents an overview of the three phases. They occur sequentially and are intimately related to one another. In this chapter, each phase is introduced with reference to an interpretive discussion that actually occurred—a discussion of Yevtushenko's poem *Schoolmaster*. The aim here is to identify the activities that take place in each phase. Later chapters will explore the activities in detail to help you understand how to develop the requisite skills and habits of mind.

PHASE 1: PREPARATION

No matter how much we prepare for it, an interpretive discussion is a spontaneous occurrence. Once the discussion begins, it flows like a river: it can be redirected, but it will go somewhere, and where it goes depends on the prior experiences, skills, and interests of the participants and leader.

While the flow of an interpretive discussion is spontaneous, it is not without form or limits, for it is a conversation about the meaning of some text. Its twofold goal is to identify some question about the meaning that the participants wish to resolve and to make progress toward its resolution. The participants and leader work together to identify the point of ambiguity. Studying the text to resolve the ambiguity becomes the focus of the conversation. The nature of the ambiguity that a group chooses to address depends on the discussants and discussion leader, who relate themselves to the text in particular ways.

The leader is critical in helping the discussants relate to the text and to one another. For one thing, the leader chooses the text, perhaps alone, perhaps as directed by others—by a curriculum, an administrator, or the discussants themselves. The choice of text involves a number of considerations, one of which is that it must be discussable. What makes a text discussable? I begin to answer the question here and consider it further in chapters 2 and 3.

In addition to selecting the text, the leader sets the tone of the discussion by coming to it as a seeker—as someone who cannot resolve, yet wishes to resolve, an ambiguity in the text. The leader teaches the discussants what it means to be a seeker by engaging them in the seeking, whereby they raise a question that they care to resolve and pursue its resolution through further study.[1]

So, what does the leader do to select a discussable text? How does he or she prepare to come to the discussion as a seeker of understanding? The answer to each of these questions requires an entire chapter in which the required skills, challenges, and habits of mind are explored in detail. Here, I only begin the stories.

Let's take the first question: What does the leader do to select a discussable text—one that can sustain discussion about its meaning for at least forty-five minutes? A text that may be discussed by one group may leave another silent. So the question becomes, How does a particular leader select a text for discussion with a particular group?

When selecting a text, the leader should consider the time set aside for the discussion, the leader's relation to the discussants, the suitability of the subject matter, and the accessibility of the work. In March 2010, I led an interpretive discussion about Yevtushenko's *Schoolmaster*. I selected *Schoolmaster* to discuss with honors sophomores at the Aurora School because I knew that I would be with them for less than one hour. The poem is short (forty lines long) and could be read in class. Since I had not met the participants previously, I needed a text to which they could quickly relate. Not only did I plan to read the poem to them, but because it explores the relation between a teacher and his students, I also believed that the discussants would find it both intriguing and familiar.

In selecting a text, the leader needs to take one more important, even critical, aspect into consideration. The text must have sufficient ambiguity to sustain conversation about its meaning. So, even though I had led discussions about the meaning of *Schoolmaster* with groups of people in the past, I needed to be sure that I still found it ambiguous. Only then could I stand on common ground with the discussants in the sense that we would all be seeking to understand its meaning together. More discussion of text selection follows in chapter 2.

So we come to the second question raised above: How does the leader prepare to come to the discussion as seeker of understanding? The solution is to locate a point of ambiguity in the text that you, the leader, wish to resolve. And the best way to do that is to write a cluster of questions about its meaning. It is also the best way I know to determine that the text is discussable—that it can sustain discussion about its meaning for at least forty-five minutes.

A cluster of questions is a set of interpretive questions—questions about the meaning of the text that may be resolved in more than one way in light of the evidence in the text. The cluster includes a basic question, which expresses the deepest point of doubt that the leader has about the meaning of the text—the question that the leader most wishes to answer. The basic question is also a one for which the leader can write eight follow-up questions, which are included in the cluster. The follow-up questions, like the basic question, are interpretive questions, that is, they are questions about the meaning of the text that can be resolved in more than one way, based upon textual evidence. In addition, the follow-up questions point to passages in the text which, if interpreted in at least one way, suggest ideas about the resolution of the basic question.

Here is the text of the Yevtushenko poem:

Schoolmaster

1   The window gives onto the white trees.
2   The master looks out of it at the trees,
3   for a long time, he looks for a long time
4   out through the window at the trees,
5   breaking his chalk slowly in one hand.
6   And it's only the rules of long division.
7   And he's forgotten the rules of long division.
8   Imagine not remembering long division!
9   A mistake on the blackboard, a mistake.
10 We watch him with a different attention
11 needing no one to hint to us about it,
12 there's more than difference in this attention.
13 The schoolmaster's wife has gone away,
14 we do not know where she has gone to,
15 we do not know why she has gone,
16 what we know is his wife has gone away.

17 His clothes are neither new nor in the fashion;
18 wearing the suit which he always wears
19 and which is neither new nor in the fashion
20 the master goes downstairs to the cloakroom.
21 He fumbles in his pocket for a ticket.
22 'What's the matter? Where is that ticket?
23 Perhaps I never picked up my ticket.
24 Where is the thing?' Rubbing his forehead.
25 'Oh, here it is. I'm getting old.
26 Don't argue Auntie Dear, I'm getting old.
27 You can't do much about getting old.'
28 We hear the door below creaking behind him.

29 The window gives onto the white trees.
30 The trees there are high and wonderful.

31   but they are not why we are looking out.

32   We look in silence at the schoolmaster.

33   He has a bent back and clumsy walk,

34   he moves without defenses, clumsily,

35   worn out I ought to have said, clumsily.

36   Snow falling on him softly through silence

37   turns him to white under the white trees.

38   He whitens into white like the trees.

39   A little longer will make him so white

40   we shall not see him in the whitened trees.

Here is the cluster of questions that I prepared for *Schoolmaster* before leading the discussion:

Basic question: Do the students watch the schoolmaster in silence (32) because they are trying to understand the effects of growing old or the effects of losing one's wife?

Follow-up questions:

1. Do the students watch the schoolmaster (32) because they feel sorry for him? If they feel sorry, is it because his wife has gone away (13–16)?
2. Do the students watch the schoolmaster (32) for the same reason they "watch him with a different attention" (10) in the classroom? If they are trying to understand the effects of aging in both cases, why do they say the schoolmaster's wife has gone away (13) after they observe his mistake on the blackboard?
3. Do the students watch the schoolmaster (32) because they think he is dying and might not return to the classroom or because they feel sorry that his wife has left him? What is it that they are "needing no one to hint to [them] about"?
4. Do the students note that the schoolmaster wears the same unfashionable suit (17–19) because this tells them he is aging?
5. Do the students imagine schoolmaster's words and actions in the cloak-room (21–28)? If so, do they do so because they are reflecting on the consequences of growing old?
6. Do the students watch the schoolmaster (32) for the same reason he watches the trees (4)? Are both students and teacher trying to understand

what happens to people when they get old, or are they trying to understand what happens to people when they lose someone they love?

7. Do the students notice that the schoolmaster has a bent back (33) because they are pondering the effects of aging? If so, does the narrator correct himself and say the schoolmaster is "worn out" (35) because he concludes that the clumsy walking comes from aging?

8. In saying, "A little longer will make him so white we shall not see him in the whitened trees" (39–40), do the students conclude that their memory of the teacher will fade as they age? Or, do they conclude that losing a loved one destroys one's desire to live?

In chapter 3, I describe the origin and development of my cluster of questions for *Schoolmaster*. Here, let us consider three features of a cluster in relation to the above example: the nature of the basic question, its relation to the follow-up questions, and the structure of the follow-up questions.

The basic question, in this particular instance, is a question about a specific line in the poem—line 32. You may be surprised that the basic question asks about a specific passage rather than the overall meaning of the poem. However, as will be discussed later in the book, the basic question may elicit more discussion when it focuses on a specific passage, as it helps discussants know where to direct their attention.

Here, the basic question asks about an event that takes place: students silently watching as their teacher leaves the school and walks out into the snow. The question assumes that the observers are students. It also suggests two possible reasons why the students may be watching in silence: perhaps they are contemplating the effects of aging, or perhaps they are contemplating the effects of losing one's wife. Those two possibilities are offered because the evidence in the poem seems to support both of them, but it is not clear which it best supports. The basic question assumes that the "we" who are watching are the schoolmaster's students, and in chapter 3, the reason for that interpretation is explained. The discussants, of course, are free to challenge the assumptions and suggestions in the question—if they can support their challenges with textual evidence.

Each follow-up question refers to some place in the poem that, if interpreted in at least one way, suggests an idea about the resolution of the basic question. Take question 1, for example: Do the students watch the schoolmaster (32) because they feel sorry for him? If they feel sorry, is it because his wife has gone away (13–16)?

The question directs attention to lines 13–16, which say that the students know that their teacher's wife has left him but that they do not know why she has left or where she has gone. Because her departure is the subject of four lines, and because lines 13 and 16 repeat the fact of her departure, I write question 1, which suggests that in answer to the basic question, the students may be watching their teacher in silence in line 32 because they are pondering the effects of losing one's wife, which makes them sad. So, the relation between the basic question and every follow-up question is very specific: the follow-up question points to a specific passage in the text—here, lines 13–16—that offers evidence for resolution of the basic question.

Our analysis of question 1 in the cluster for *Schoolmaster* suggests that a follow-up question has a particular structure. Specifically, it (1) identifies a particular passage, (2) interprets the passage, and (3) suggests an idea about the resolution of the basic question, based on the interpretation of the passage. You may see that other questions in the cluster generally have the same structure. However, while each question points to particular passages in the text and suggests ideas about the resolution of the basic question according to an interpretation of them, the interpretation of the passages is not always explicit. In chapter 3, we explore criteria that may be used to evaluate and clarify the questions.

Once a prepared cluster meets certain criteria of clarity (described in chapter 3), the leader can be confident that the text is discussable. That confidence arises when the leader identifies a point of ambiguity that the participants may address by studying at least eight places in the text that suggest ideas about its resolution. Having written a cluster of questions, the leader enters the discussion as a seeker of understanding, knowing that the question can be addressed by further study of the text—a study that generally lasts forty-five minutes or more.

In summary, the preparation phase of interpretive discussion includes the selection of a text that is suitable for the discussion, given the circumstances. The text must also be discussable, meaning that the leader feels sufficient ambiguity about its meaning. Furthermore, the leader must enter the discussion as a seeker of understanding about the meaning of the text. To become a seeker and to verify that the text is discussable, the leader needs to develop a cluster of questions about it.[2]

PHASE 2: LEADING THE DISCUSSION

After preparing a cluster of questions, how does the leader help the participants form a shared point of doubt about the meaning of the text and make progress toward resolution? In chapters 4, 5, and 6, we consider excerpts from three discussions to address the question. We study the skills and habits of mind that are required for and developed by leading interpretive discussion. We see not only what the leader does but also how the discussants respond to the leader's efforts.

To begin our study of discussion leading, let us look at the opening of the *Schoolmaster* discussion that I led at the Aurora School. The leader has just finished reading the poem and learning the names of the fourteen discussants.[3] She gives them the choice of beginning with their questions or the basic question she has prepared. They select the latter, and so she poses it:

> SHG: All right, line 32, okay? So, Michael, when we look at line 32, okay? Line 32 says, "We look in silence at the schoolmaster." Now, do the students watch the schoolmaster in silence at line 32 because they are trying to understand the effects of growing old or because they are trying to understand the effects of losing one's life?

The question seems to be clear. But will these discussants find it of interest and wish to address it? Will Michael recognize that the leader is inviting him into the conversation and respond easily, or will he feel anxious—put on the spot—and hesitate to speak?

> MICHAEL: Well, when I looked at line 32, the first thing I see, I see a reversal. I see a parallel to the schoolmaster looking out on the white … the white trees, whereas in line 32 now I see the schoolchildren looking out at the schoolmaster almost becoming part of the white trees.

Here, Michael speaks without hesitation. Furthermore, he puts his attention on line 32 of the text, much as the question directs him to do. However, he does not answer the question. In saying, "When I looked at line 32 … I see a reversal," he says what he sees in the line, but he does not explain why the students "watch the schoolmaster in silence." He does not choose either of the options offered; nor does he suggest another one. And what does he mean by "a reversal"? The leader tries to find out:

SHG: So line 32 is the children looking out at the schoolmaster. And what's the line where … the other line?

MICHAEL: Line 2.

SHG: Line 2, okay, where the master looks out at the trees.

Whatever a "reversal" is, the leader now knows that Michael sees something in the text that made him use the word. And if there is evidence for it in the text, then one has hope of grasping what he means by it as well as something about his view of the text. Fortunately, he proceeds to explain his thinking:

MICHAEL: Exactly. So, when I compare those two lines, I see the reversal between the schoolmaster and the children. It's almost as if the children take the place of the schoolmaster. So, as the poem wraps up to close and it's almost as if the schoolmaster becomes absorbed in the trees or becomes part of the trees. I see it more as though … the students are observing, I guess, the decline of the schoolmaster, I guess, harkening back to the second stanza, in which he's unable to find his ticket, and in the first stanza, he's unable … or he makes a mistake on the blackboard, seemingly because his wife has left. It's as if this great being that we're introduced with in the first two lines is declining throughout the poem.

When Michael says, "So, when I compare those two lines I see the reversal between the schoolmaster and the children. It's almost as if the children take the place of the school master," he may mean that in line 2, the schoolmaster is looking out the window and watching, whereas in line 32, the students are looking out—they have taken the place of the schoolmaster at the window. So a "reversal" may mean that characters have changed places with respect to location.

But Michael does not stop here. Indeed, as he continues, he leaves the observation that the students and teacher have traded places in front of the window. When he says, "So, as the poem wraps up to close and it's almost as if the schoolmaster becomes absorbed in the trees or becomes part of the trees," he directs attention to the end of the poem. He does not mention line numbers, but he seems to be interpreting something, perhaps the last lines of the poem, 36–40, when he says, "It's almost as if the schoolmaster becomes absorbed in the trees or becomes part of the trees." He then adds, "I see it more as though … the students are observing, I guess, the decline of the schoolmaster."

A listener might feel as if Michael has a question on his mind that he wishes to address. However, it is not the one that the leader posed initially—why the students watch the schoolmaster in silence at line 32. Instead, his question seems to be, What is this poem about? When he directs attention to "the close" of the poem saying, "And it's almost as if the schoolmaster becomes absorbed in the trees or becomes part of the trees. I see it more as though ... the students are observing, I guess, the decline of the schoolmaster," he explains that the poem is about students watching their teacher fade into the landscape—"the trees"—which Michael seems to see as a metaphor for declining.

Michael continues to speak, now offering additional textual evidence to support his position. When he says, "I guess, harkening back to the second stanza, in which he's unable to find his ticket, and in the first stanza, he's unable ... or he makes a mistake on the blackboard," he seems to mean that the schoolmaster's inability to locate his ticket, as indicated in stanza 2, and his mathematical mistake on the blackboard, as indicated in stanza 1, show that he is "declining."

Michael has even more to say: "Or he [the schoolmaster] makes a mistake on the blackboard, seemingly because his wife has left." In so saying, Michael again shifts the question on the floor. He seems anxious to explain why the schoolmaster made the error on the blackboard, not what the poem is about. He marches on to answer his new query: "Seemingly because his wife has gone away." The answer he offers refers to textual evidence (lines 13–16 of the poem), although he does not mention specific line numbers. His use of the word "seemingly" suggests that he is unsure about whether the wife's departure caused the teacher to err.

Michael continues: "It's as if this great being that we're introduced with in the first two lines is declining throughout the poem." Here, he seems to return to the first question he raised and his initial response: he may be saying that the poem is about the teacher's—the "great being's"—loss of cognitive capacity and perhaps more.

Now, look where we are. Initially, the leader asked Michael, "Do the students watch the schoolmaster in silence at line 32 because they are trying to understand the effects of growing old or because they are trying to understand the effects of losing one's life?" This is a question about what concerns the students as they watch their schoolmaster walk out into the snow. Subsequently, Michael shifts to the question of what the poem is about, as argued above. When he says that the schoolmaster "makes a mistake on the blackboard, seemingly because his wife has left," Michael shifts the question again and now tries to explain why the schoolmaster made the mistake on the blackboard (line 9). When he finishes speaking, does Michael still wonder what the poem is about? Or is he more interested in why the schoolmaster makes a mathematical error on the blackboard? And what about the prepared basic question that the leader has posed initially?

While leading a discussion, a leader may sometimes sense his or her own failure to grasp the participant's meaning. In the above excerpts, you can also sense that the question on the floor is shifting. In general, such movement is a good thing, for only as the question shifts does the group grope toward a question that it cares to resolve. Indeed, that question may be very different from the one posed initially. To succeed, a leader needs to recognize the question being addressed at all times, and if more than one question has been raised, the leader must direct the conversation in one way or another. If the question or what has been said is unclear, it is the leader's job to help bring about clarification. It is also up to the leader to guide the group in a direction that helps the shared point of doubt to form and become resolved. Fortunately, by leading and reflecting on interpretive discussions over time, leaders can develop the skills and habits of mind needed for appropriate response.

In chapter 4, we will see how the leader responded when, after Michael's comments, there were three questions before the group and not one. For now, let us turn to the third phase of interpretive discussion—reflection.

PHASE 3: REFLECTION

The reflection phase of an interpretive discussion takes place once the discussion concludes. I do not mean to imply that reflection is missing from preparation and leading; indeed quite the contrary. However, I distinguish between reflection and the reflection phase. The term *reflection* I borrow from John Dewey, who presents a classic definition:

> When a situation arises containing a difficulty, or perplexity, the person who finds himself in it … may face the situation. In this case, he begins to reflect. The moment he begins to reflect, he begins of necessity to observe in order to take stock of conditions [to] … get as clear and distinct a recognition as possible of the nature of the situation with which he has to deal …

[S]uggestions arise of possible courses of action ... the mind leaps forward to a possible solution. [He develops] an intellectualization of the difficulty ... that has been *felt* into a *problem* to be solved. [He uses] one suggestion as a leading idea or *hypothesis*, eventually *testing* the hypothesis.[4]

Thus, according to Dewey, reflection takes place when a person encounters an obstacle in the course of some activity. The obstacle must be surmounted if the activity is to continue, but the nature of the obstacle is not always clear at the outset. The first step of reflection, as Dewey indicates, is to consider the features of the obstacle until it can be formulated as a problem. Once the problem is clearly defined, ideas about its resolution can be generated. And once possible solutions have been identified, one solution or more may be selected for testing. Reflection, so defined, may take place in any phase of interpretive discussion, provided a person stops the normal course of action to follow the steps that Dewey outlines.

Donald Schön, in the classic work *Educating the Reflective Practitioner*, recognized that reflection must sometimes take place in the course of activities.[5] Sometimes, the situation does not permit the practitioner to engage in the sustained, systematic thinking that Dewey describes. Schön gives examples of musicians, artists, and others who must make decisions about how to overcome obstacles very quickly, sometimes instantaneously. All of them must execute "reflection in action": "Often a problematic situation presents itself as a unique case. The case is not 'in the book.' If [a person] is to deal with it competently, [he or she] must do so by a kind of improvisation, inventing and testing in the situation strategies of [the person's] own devising."[6]

Certainly, leaders of interpretive discussion fall into the category of those who must practice reflection in action during their activities. As we will see, the leader's response to Michael in the discussion of *Schoolmaster* required just that, as the student made several complex remarks that had to be managed then and there if a shared question about the meaning of the poem was to emerge in the group.

So there is reflection, and there is reflection in action. Phase 3 of the interpretive discussion, what I call the reflection phase, takes place after the discussion concludes. It is not reflection in action. On the contrary, the reflection phase requires removal from the action of leading.

In general, leaders (with or without discussants) begin the reflection phase by asking themselves, Did a shared point of doubt arise—a question that most if not all in the group wished to resolve? If it did not arise, then why not? If it did arise, what was it? And how did it arise from what was said? These questions prompt the reflection that follows.

For example, we have seen that at the point when Michael finishes his remarks, there are three questions on the floor: First, do the students watch the schoolmaster in silence at line 32 because they are trying to understand the effects of growing old or because they are trying to understand the effects of losing one's wife? (the leader's basic question). Second, what is the poem about? And third, why does the schoolmaster make a mathematical error on the blackboard? Now, one of these questions may become of interest to others such that more discussants work to answer it. Another question may also arise, once other participants, or even Michael himself, begin to answer one of the three questions. Or an entirely different question might be posed even before any of the three suggested thus far is taken up. During the reflection phase, the leader traces the content of the conversation to clarify where the shared question came from if indeed it formed.

The reflection phase also looks at the content of the conversation to determine the progress made toward resolution of that shared point of doubt. For example, suppose the reflection on the *Schoolmaster* discussion revealed that the shared question became, What is the poem about? If that was the question that most people tried to address in the conversation, then we would want to see what was said about the answer to it. We would also want to see if the question remained in that form or was revised. Michael's comments suggest that even in posing the issue of what the poem is about, he offered an idea about its resolution. When he says, "I see it more as though … the students are observing, I guess, the decline of the schoolmaster," and then adds, "It's as if this great being that we're introduced with in the first two lines is declining throughout the poem." In so saying, he suggests that in answer to his question, the poem is about the schoolmaster's becoming less in some way—"declining."

Sometimes, a shared point of doubt does not form. Because we observe only part of the Yevtushenko discussion, as the video recording was incomplete, we can see a shared question emerging. We cannot see that all the participants wish to address it. In other cases that we consider later in the book, we see the shared point of doubt form gradually. It is important to determine why the group fails to come to a shared question, or fails to do it quickly. The reasons can be various. Once you begin to recognize the conditions that favor the formation of a shared question, you can work to create these conditions.

During the reflection phase, leaders can see that by following certain discussion-leading and listening patterns, they help their groups form and address shared points of doubt. For example, let's look again at the opening of the discussion of *Schoolmaster*. Although the dialogue has thus far been between the leader and one participant, both people follow patterns that, over the course of the discussion, help a shared question to develop.

> SHG: All right, line 32, okay? So, Michael, when we look at line 32, okay? Line 32 says, "We looked in silence at the schoolmaster." Now, do the students watch the schoolmaster in silence at line 32 because they are trying to understand the effects of growing old or because they are trying to understand the effects of losing one's wife?

Here, we see four patterns that discussion leaders typically follow. First, they often pose a basic question that has been prepared before the discussion begins. Second, they often direct it toward a particular participant, being careful to mention the name before posing the question so that the discussant can prepare himself or herself to answer. Here, the prepared basic question directs attention to a particular aspect of the text by mentioning a page or line number. In addition, the question begins to interpret the text by suggesting an idea about its meaning. So, instead of asking why the students look in silence at the schoolmaster (line 32), the question asks whether they do so because they are trying to understand the effect of aging or losing one's wife. Michael, to whom the question was directed, responded:

> MICHAEL: Well, when I looked at line 32, the first thing I see, I see a reversal. I see a parallel to the schoolmaster looking out on the white … the white trees, whereas in line 32 now I see the schoolchildren looking out at the schoolmaster almost becoming part of the white trees.

As indicated previously, Michael responded without hesitation, but he does not answer the question. As the leader did not fully comprehend Michael's response, she followed his comment with a third discussion-leading pattern—one that is typically observed in such circumstances:

> SHG: So line 32 is the children looking out at the schoolmaster. And what's the line where … the other line?

MICHAEL: Line 2.

SHG: Line 2, okay, where the master looks out at the trees.

Here, the leader asks Michael to identify specific places in the text that provoked his idea. He mentions the evidence in line 2. In so doing, he responds with a listening pattern, that is, a response that is typically given by participants when defending their claims about the meaning of the text. They cite specific places in the text that provide evidence for the idea, such as line or page numbers or other indicators of specific locations on a page. In following the expected listening pattern, Michael responds in the way the leader intended him to respond.[7] The leader then follows with another common discussion-leading pattern: that of repeating what a discussant says so as to confirm understanding of his intended meaning. Michael follows by focusing attention on the lines that suggest to him that a "reversal" is taking place.

As Michael continues, he does something very interesting: He almost initiates discussion-leading patterns that the leader had initiated previously. Even though he does not mention line numbers or directly quote the poem, Michael directs the discussion to a recognizable location in the text: "So, as the poem wraps up to close and it's almost as if the schoolmaster becomes absorbed in the trees or becomes part of the trees."

Furthermore, when he adds, "I see it more as though … the students are observing, I guess, the decline of the schoolmaster," he interprets the portion of the text to which he drew attention. When posing the basic question initially, the leader asked, "Do the students watch the schoolmaster in silence at line 32 because they are trying to understand the effects of growing old or because they are trying to understand the effects of losing one's wife?" Not only does the question point to a specific line in the text (line 32), but as indicated above, it also suggests ideas about what the students may have been pondering as they watched the schoolmaster walk out into the snow. Likewise, instead of asking, What is this poem about? Michael suggests an answer by saying that it is about the "decline" of the schoolmaster. Much as the leader has done previously in posing the basic question, Michael suggests an interpretation of the text to which he draws attention.

Not yet finished, Michael next points to more textual evidence. When he says, "I guess harkening back to the second stanza in which he's unable to find his ticket and in the first stanza, he's unable … or he makes a mistake on the blackboard," Michael, again of his own volition, directs attention to sections of the text. One might argue that that his reference to the text is more specific now, as he mentions particular events that occurred in the poem (losing ticket; mistake on blackboard). However, he again fails to give line numbers, which means his reference to the text is less precise than it might be.

Likewise, when he says, "seemingly because his wife has left. It's as if this great being that we're introduced with within the first two lines is declining throughout the poem," Michael suggests two ideas about the meaning of nonspecific aspects of the text. In the first instance, he opines that the schoolmaster may have made a mistake on the blackboard and maybe even lost his ticket because his wife has departed from him. As Michael continues, he argues that losing the ticket and making a mistake on the blackboard indicate that the poem is about "this great being"—the schoolmaster—declining as the students watch. In both instances, Michael initiates interpretation of the text, but the reference is still somewhat vague, as he does not mention specific line numbers.

As we will see, the reference to specific places in a text using page and line numbers makes possible clearer, more productive, more interesting, and more satisfying discussions. Still in all, even in his opening comments, we see Michael moving toward closer study of the details of Yevtushenko's poem.

The foregoing analysis shows a leader following certain discussion-leading patterns. She began the discussion by posing a basic question developed previously, which immediately gave the group a possible point of focus. She addressed it to a particular speaker. As in this example, the question may ask directly about the meaning of lines or phrases in the text and may suggest interpretations for the participants to consider. As the discussion progressed, the leader asked for textual evidence and repeated back what she understood the discussant to mean. Later in the book, we will see that by following these patterns, the leader helps to move the discussants toward shared points of doubts and helps the group make progress toward the resolution of these points.

Understanding productive discussion-leading patterns and when to use them requires skill and the development of certain habits of mind. Fortunately, that understanding and habituation are acquired through the experience of preparing for, leading, and reflecting on interpretive discussion.

Yet, no matter how skillful and experienced they are, leaders will not succeed until and unless the participants are following appropriate listening patterns and in time, initiating appropriate discussion-leading patterns themselves. We have seen Michael begin to do both. He responded with the number of a line that offered evidence for his idea of reversal; he also drew attention to sections of the text and suggested interpretations of them. By so doing, Michael begins to form a question that interests him and to offer ideas about the answer. That question may be one that others come to share.

In actual practice, leaders and discussants may not study a transcript of the discussion during the reflection phase. They need not necessarily do so. They may be able to recognize and recall productive discussion-leading and listening patterns and to connect the use of these patterns to the content of the conversation to understand why it developed as it did. In chapter 4, productive discussion-leading patterns are identified in discussion excerpts, and the suitability of the discussants' listening patterns will be apparent. In chapters 5 and 6, the productive patterns become even more evident as we peruse excerpts from discussions of "Rats" and Toni Morrison's Nobel Laureate lecture. Once the value of these patterns becomes clear to leaders and participants, they follow the patterns—just as Michael is beginning to do. They also become increasingly skillful in so doing.

SUMMARY

In this chapter, I have introduced the three phases of interpretive discussion: preparation, leading, and reflection. (For a quick review of the three phases, please see appendixes A and B.) Successful leading requires skills and habits of mind that are cultivated in each of the three phases. With careful preparation, leaders identify a discussable text. By developing a cluster of questions, they not only certify the text as discussable, but also bring themselves to the discussions with their students ready to learn with them about the meaning of the text. As fellow seekers leading the discussion, the leaders follow patterns that not only engage the discussants but also teach them to participate with increasing effectiveness. In identifying and pursuing resolution of a shared point of doubt, both leaders and participants follow the productive leading and listening patterns and, in so doing, develop the requisite skills and habits of mind. Finally, the reflection phase allows recognition of what the discussion has accomplished in terms of the content of the conversation, particularly with reference to the formation of a shared point of doubt and the progress toward resolution. The reflection phase also gives the leader an opportunity to ponder the growth of the individuals' skills and habits of mind, and the formation of the group as a productive, collaborative community.

Part 1 looks at the preparation phase of interpretive discussion. Part 2 takes up the other two phases—leading and reflection—after presenting excerpts from the discussions. So now, let us turn to closer study of the preparation phase, beginning with the topic of text selection.

Preparation

2

Selecting a Text

INTERPRETIVE DISCUSSION is appropriate for students in kindergarten through graduate school and in many subject areas. How can one instructional orientation be suitable for such a wide variety of ages and subject matters? The reason is that in every case, there is a text that the group works to interpret. If the text meets certain criteria, which will be laid out in this chapter, then an interpretive discussion of it can be highly productive. Although you need more than just an appropriate text for a successful interpretive discussion, you cannot have such a discussion without the right text. And although it may seem surprising, even young children are capable of text interpretation.[1]

In the previous chapter, I defined a discussable text as one that can sustain conversation about its meaning for forty-five minutes. Now we'll explore what is meant by a *text*. In order to discuss the meaning of a text, the leader and participants must follow some rules of various sorts. We'll look at the three texts that will be further explored in later chapters and think about the rules required in each instance. By so doing, we gain insight into what is required for text interpretation. We also see how points of ambiguity arise from following the rules—ambiguities that may become basic questions in cluster preparations or shared points of doubt in interpretive discussions.

WHAT IS A TEXT?

In *Learning to Teach Through Discussion: The Art of Turning the Soul*, I define a text that is suitable for interpretive discussion as "any item with enough ambiguity to permit questioning of its meaning … a story or other work of fiction, nonfiction … a relic or artifact (Stonehenge, a totem pole) … a data set, film, photograph, a painting, musical composition, or an example of architecture … In general, a text is delimited in some way."[2]

According to the above definition, a text is some object, and it is only discussable if the readers-observers can find ambiguity in it. The discussion that transpires aims to resolve the ambiguity.[3] Indeed, if there are no questions about the meaning of a text, so that the meaning is clear or cannot be clarified by further study of it, then there is nothing to discuss until the text is left behind or related to another object of some sort.[4]

The definition of the term *ambiguity* I take from William Empson: "any verbal nuance, however slight, which gives room for alternative reactions to the same piece of language."[5] Empson offers seven types of ambiguity but, in general, seems to have in mind the situation in which some passage or element in the text may have more than one meaning, given the textual evidence. So how is it that readers-observers identify ambiguity? That is, how do they determine that different meanings of a text are possible, given other things that appear in it?

The British sociolinguist M. A. K. Halliday asserts that a text is some object that has meaning for the observer.[6] The meaning is present because the observer, looking at the object, can follow rules. That is, when looking at the text, the observer can say to himself or herself, "When I look at this object, I see condition *a*, which means that condition *b* is also the case." For example, when I peruse *Alice in Wonderland*, I see that Alice is a character, which means to me that she will have some adventures in the story. By following rules, an author presents characters with particular features and relations to other characters. The readers-observers must be able to follow the rules that have been followed in the text if they want to interpret the text.

Halliday says that three categories of rules are followed in creating a text: (1) the semantic, that is, rules that create the meaning; (2) the lexico-grammatical rules that create the wording of the text (syntax, morphology, and lexis); and (3) the phonological rules, or those that create the sound. Our focus will be on the first kind of rules, those that create the meaning. The semantic rules are split into three further categories. The first are the ideational rules, or those concerning the content—what the text is about. These include experiential rules, or those that govern the action or experience that takes place, and the logical rules, or those that govern relations between actions, events, and actors. The second category, the interpersonal rules, govern the relations between characters in the text. The third category includes the textual rules, including those related to themes in the text. The text as a whole is governed by rules of genre (poems, narrative prose, scientific analysis, etc.), structure, and the situation of the author.[7]

In a story, for example, the author follows rules to present the actors, the things they do, the location of their activities, and the relations between the characters. Rules of logic are invoked to create necessary or possible relations between the characters, their actions, and the locations in which the actions occur. There are also rules that define the theme or themes of the text and its focus—the theme of power and the tensions between characters that the power creates, for example.[8]

As Halliday states, "a text is the product of its environment and functions in that environment."[9] The "environment" of a text includes its genre—whether it is a poem, a story, a film, a set of statistical data, an artifact, and so on—as well as the setting, the time and place of its creation, and the cultural practices of the creator. The nature and meaning of the text will be related to these factors.[10]

So how does ambiguity arise for a reader-observer looking at a text? It arises when the observer follows the rules that have been followed in presenting the text. A discussable text is one whose rules the leader and discussants can follow, and in following the rules, they detect points of ambiguity that they then discuss—points at which they say, "We see that condition *a* holds in the text, but does that mean that condition *b* or *c* also holds?" For example, we see that Alice is a character in the story of *Alice in Wonderland*, but is she more powerful than the Queen of Hearts, or is she less powerful?

SELECTING A TEXT

One way to select a text is to ask, Can the reader-observer follow the rules exhibited in the text and thereby find points of ambiguity in it—points of ambiguity that, if resolved through discussion, permit the discovery of meaning in it? Let us now look at three texts and the rules needed to interpret them. In so doing, we gain further insight into how ambiguity arises and, thus, how a discussable text is selected.

Schoolmaster, by Yevgeny Yevtushenko

If *Schoolmaster* is suitable for interpretive discussion by a group, the leader and the discussants need to be able to see that according to the text, the schoolmaster is a character who looks out the window at the white trees (line 2), for example. Likewise, they must be able to see that the "we" mentioned in line 32 are those who silently watch the schoolmaster out the window as he walks out in the snow. In other words, they need to be able to identify facts presented by the text.

Furthermore, they need to recognize that the schoolmaster may be less knowledgeable than the students with respect to the rules of long division. The poem says that he has forgotten the rules of long division (7) and that he has made a mistake at the blackboard (9). Furthermore, he also may not be living with his wife, as his "wife has gone away" (13 and 16). These conclusions about the relations between the schoolmaster and the other characters in the poem follow logically, given the information presented.

In addition, the leader and the participants need to understand that a theme of the poem may be that of aging and its effects. The schoolmaster says, "'I am getting old … You can't do much about getting old'" (25–28). The narrator says of the schoolmaster, "He has a bent back and a clumsy walk, he moves without defenses, clumsily, worn out I ought to have said" (33–35). These and other lines in the poem present evidence that at least one theme of the poem is that of aging.

Let's try some rule following to see what happens. Read the first two lines of *Schoolmaster*: "The window gives onto the white trees. The master looks out of it at the trees." From these lines, you can learn that the white trees are seen by a schoolmaster or teacher, that the teacher is a character in the poem, and that he is engaged in looking out a window at white trees. As the trees that the schoolmaster watches are "white," you might ask, Is the teacher looking at winter outside? And why is he looking out the window at the trees instead of teaching? Indeed, why does he look "for a long time out through the window at the trees" (3–4)? Why does he break his chalk instead of writing with it on the blackboard, and break it slowly as if deliberately (5)?

As you keep reading, answers to these questions are suggested by the text. For example, line 7 says, "And he's forgotten the rules of long division." Perhaps the teacher is looking out the window rather than teaching because he is unable to teach long division, which must have been his subject, since we are told that "he's forgotten the rules." And maybe he looks for a long time because he is thinking—thinking about his loss of memory. Does he break his chalk because he is impatient with himself for forgetting?

By following the rules and identifying characters, their actions, the locations of the actions, and the relations between the characters, for example, you engage in a dialectical activity. You move back and forth between what you see in a text, which sets up expectations in the form of questions about what is taking place at a given point and what is yet to come. As Wolfgang Iser, a reader-response theorist puts it, the goal of reading is to build a consistent understanding of the text.[11] Hence, in interpreting a text, the reader follows rules, and in so doing, questions and possible answers continue to arise. Let's keep going.

Line 7 says, "And he's forgotten the rules of long division." Who is speaking here? An omniscient narrator? Someone in the classroom observing the schoolmaster? Or is the schoolmaster thinking about himself, talking about himself in the third person? Thus far, it could be any of these possibilities, and so we have a possible point of ambiguity. Lines 8 and 9 could be spoken by any of the three, so they do not put the question to rest.

However, line 10 says, "We watch him with a different attention." Does the "we" refer to observers in the classroom, perhaps the students? Or does it refer to the narrator plus the reader? It could refer to either, it seems. However, it does not seem to refer to the schoolmaster himself. If he were speaking, he would not say, "We watch him." Line 10 suggests that the speaker is not the schoolmaster. But is it instead an omniscient narrator who can both observe and read thoughts? Or is it more than one observer, where one of them speaks for many? And are the many—the "we"—the students in the classroom? Do they watch their teacher with a "different attention" because they see him making mistakes and they begin to wonder why he was making them?

The latter possibility seems to be confirmed by lines 11 and 12. When they say, "Needing no one to hint to us about it," it may mean that the students not only notice and ponder the teacher's change in behavior but also need no hint about why it is taking place. Perhaps in lines 13–16, the "we" means the students, who explain their hypothesis: they know that the schoolmaster's wife has left him, and that's why he is distracted and making mistakes.

However, the ambiguity about who the speaker is arises again in the second stanza of the poem. Lines 17–20 could well have been spoken by the students, or one student, reporting the observation of all the students in the classroom. But then we get to line 21, "He fumbles in his pocket for a ticket." How can the students continue to "observe" the schoolmaster if he has gone downstairs (20) and they are still upstairs? Do they begin to report their imaginings from here until line 27? Or is the speaker not a student reporting student observations but an omniscient narrator who observes the conversation taking place between the schoolmaster and "Auntie Dear"?

As mentioned earlier, if a text is discussable, then the leaders and participants are able to follow rules and, in so doing, to find meaning in it. At the same time, we can see that through the rule following, people identify points of ambiguity, which can be discussed to clarify the meaning.

If ambiguity emerges when the rules of a text are followed, then selecting a text for discussion involves trying to follow its rules—to understand it—and in so doing, uncovering points of ambiguity or points at which the language of the text could mean one thing or another. If the text is discussable, then the questions about its meaning can be addressed by further study of the text. So an interpretive discussion is focused on careful exploration of passages that may seem to eliminate the perceived ambiguities.

The text must be sufficiently ambiguous to sustain forty-five minutes of discussion about its meaning. In chapter 3, we explore the test for identifying sufficient ambiguity in a text. Before so doing, however, let me introduce two other texts whose meaning was discussed by groups we will meet in subsequent chapters. What do the rules look like in these instances—one a scientific essay and the other a speech? And do you uncover ambiguity in the same way that you do with a fictional case, such as *Schoolmaster?*

"Rats," by Konrad Lorenz

The second case we consider is one in which a class of seventh-grade science students discussed "Rats," a reading by Konrad Lorenz (1903–1989), founder of the comparative study of animal behavior (ethology).[12] In leading the discussion, I was joined by a graduate of the teacher preparation program at Northwestern University and a former student.[13] I call her Ms. Prentice. She is an experienced science teacher, but she was new to the middle school where the discussion occurred. She told me that she had not yet engaged her students there in interpretive discussion but wanted to try it. As she was teaching biology, she asked me to suggest a biology text for the discussion. Again, I wanted something relatively short that would interest the students.

As it turned out, the text we used was challenging. Nevertheless, the students made progress in identifying a shared point of doubt. Although moving toward resolution was somewhat difficult, as we will see in chapter 5, progress nevertheless transpired.

The text is a three-page excerpt from chapter 10 of Lorenz's famous work, *On Aggression*, published in 1963 (see appendix C for the entire excerpt). The excerpt opens as follows:

Rats

1 Serious fights between members of
2 the same big family [of rats] occur in one situation only, which in many
3 respects is significant and interesting: such fights take place when a strange
4 rat is present and has aroused intraspecific, interfamily aggression. What
5 rats do when a member of a strange rat clan enters their territory or is put
6 in there by a human experimenter is one of the most horrible and repulsive
7 things which can be observed in animals. The strange rat may run around
8 for minutes on end without having any idea of the terrible fate awaiting it,
9 and the resident rats may continue for an equally long time with their ordi-
10 nary affairs till finally the stranger comes close enough to one of them for
11 it to get wind of the intruder. The information is transmitted like an electric
12 shock through the resident rat, and at once the whole colony is alarmed by
13 a process of mood transmission which is communicated in the brown rat
14 by expression movements but in the house rat by a sharp, shrill, satanic cry
15 which is taken up by all members of the tribe within earshot.
16 With their eyes bulging from their sockets, their hair standing on end,
17 the rats set out on the rat hunt.

Here, we have a nonfictional text—a quasi research report that includes descriptions of observed phenomena. In order to locate points of ambiguity in the text, the reader begins just as he or she would begin in viewing the Yevtushenko text, namely, by trying to follow the rules that are exhibited in the text. But what does it mean to "follow the rules" in reading the Lorenz excerpt?

When it says that "serious fights" occur between members of the same "big" family of rats (lines 1–2), we learn that if X is a character in the text, then X is a rat. Furthermore, if Xs are rats, then they exist within "families." And within "big" families, the rats fight one another. If the reader is not familiar with the concepts of rats or families or fighting, the text might have little meaning. And even if you know these concepts, what is meant by a "big" family of rats? Already, a question has arisen.

Furthermore, when the text says that fights between rats occur when a "strange rat" appears among the group (lines 3–4), the reader learns that if X is a character in the text, then X is either a "strange rat" or a "resident rat." The reader is told that acts of aggression—fighting—occur when the strange rat arouses "intraspecific, interfamily aggression" (4). What does that phrase mean?

Thus, by trying to identify the characters in the text, their actions, the locations of the actions, and the relations between the characters, the reader identifies the characters as rats of two kinds (strange and resident) and learns that the action takes place when a strange rat arouses the aggressive response of the resident rats. Because it is a research report, the characters are not expected to have individual personalities or traits, as the schoolmaster does in Yevtushenko's poem.

In following the rules to understand the text, you might wonder, Do the so-called strange rats belong to the same "big" family as the resident rats but to a different subfamily or clan? And under what conditions does the strange rat arouse an aggressive response in the resident rats? Lines 5–7 indicate that the aggressive response occurs when the strange rat "enters their [others'] territory": it locates itself in a place occupied by resident rats. But as you read on, more ideas and questions arise.

For example, when the text says, "The strange rat may run around for minutes on end without having any idea of the terrible fate awaiting it" (7–8), does it mean that the strange rat does not intend to fight the others? Is its only offense somehow arriving in foreign territory? And does "intraspecific, interfamily aggression"

(4) mean fighting that occurs within (*intra*) the space of one rat clan but between (*inter*) members of more than one clan? Is the "stranger" (10) the "intruder" (11)? Is the "brown rat" (13) another name for the strange rat, or could it be any of the rats—strange or resident? If the former, do both the strange and the resident rats change when the strange rat is recognized as such? That is, do the resident rats give "a sharp, shrill, satanic cry" (14), and does the strange rat show "expression movements" (14)?

Here we see that as we try to follow the rules exhibited in the text, apparent ambiguities arise—ambiguities about the referents for the names of the characters, their actions, and the relations between them. In fact, the presence of these apparent ambiguities has a great impact on the discussion that we observe in chapter 5.

Ms. Prentice and I decided to divide her class so that ten students discussed the text while the others observed, and then the observers became the participants and the participants the observers. Both groups of discussants struggled to resolve questions about who the characters were and what they did. However, the second group moved on to take up a point of doubt that it did not easily resolve—a question for which more than one resolution is possible, given the textual evidence. Indeed, it is a question that Lorenz himself expresses: "What is the purpose of group hate between rat clans?" (line 54; see appendix C). In the section of the text that follows, he puzzles over the answer to the question:

65   It is not impossible
66   that as-yet unknown external selection factors are still at work; we can, how-
67   ever, maintain with certainty that those indispensable species-preserving
68   functions of intraspecific aggression … are not served by clan fights. These
69   serve neither spatial distribution nor the selection of strong family defend-
70   ers—for among rats these are seldom the fathers of the descendants …

By trying to follow the rules that are exhibited in the text, we begin to understand what Lorenz means when he asks, "What is the purpose of group hate between rat clans?" (line 54; see appendix C). When he says, "indispensable species-preserving functions of intraspecific aggression … are not served by clan fights" (line 67–68), he may mean that fighting between groups of rats within large families—"rat clans"—does not help preserve rats as a species. Thus, the "purpose" he has in mind is survival. Here, the purpose is one we might expect an ethologist to consider. The "environment" of the text—including the kind of text it is, namely, an analysis of animal (rat) behavior—brings to bear kinds of rules that identify the actors as rats, their actions as acts of aggression with certain territories, the relations between the actors as hostile relations between resident and strange rats, for example.[14] Knowing the environment of the text allows us to see that by his question, Lorenz means, How is the survival of the species (rats) furthered by the hatred that exists between rats of different rat clans?

When Lorenz continues by saying, "These [fights between the rat clans] serve neither spatial distribution nor the selection of strong family defenders, for among rats these are seldom the fathers of the descendants" (68–70), he clarifies his point of doubt. He is saying that the fights neither help the rats find unoccupied territory ("special distribution") nor insure that the most aggressive rats within a family will reproduce, as those individuals will be most likely to die in combat. So how can fights between clans of rats help the species of rats to survive? That is his dilemma—the point of doubt he wishes to resolve.

As we will see in chapter 5, which analyzes the seventh-grade science class's discussion of "Rats," the students begin to grasp and share the point of doubt that preoccupied Lorenz himself. As a consequence, they begin to worry about a central concept of evolutionary theory: natural selection. Furthermore, despite the challenges presented by the text, or perhaps because of them, the students begin to acquire practices and habits of mind that, when developed, can help them interpret texts successfully.

Nobel Laureate Speech, Delivered by Toni Morrison

As detailed in chapter 6, a group of fourteen high school seniors and I discuss the meaning of a speech that Toni Morrison gave in 1993, when she received the Nobel Prize in Literature in Stockholm, Sweden.[15] The speech in its entirety appears in appendix D. It is a dense work of 215 lines—one that was not easy for either the discussants or me to interpret. The group struggles to follow the rules that govern the text. Eventually, the students make progress with the rule following and come to a question they care to resolve as they uncover a point of ambiguity in the work. They also make progress resolving the question.

Morrison frames her speech around a story:

11   Once upon a time there was an old woman. Blind. Wise.

12   In the version I know the woman is the daughter of slaves, black, American,
      and lives

13   alone in a small house outside of town. Her reputation for wisdom is without
      peer and

14   without question. Among her people she is both the law and its
      transgression. The honor

15   she is paid and the awe in which she is held reach beyond her
      neighborhood to places far

16   away; to the city where the intelligence of rural prophets is the source of much

17   amusement.

18   One day the woman is visited by some young people who seem to be bent
      on disproving

19   her clairvoyance and showing her up for the fraud they believe she is. Their
      plan is

20   simple: they enter her house and ask the one question the answer to which
      rides solely on

21   her difference from them, a difference they regard as a profound disability:
      her blindness.

22   They stand before her, and one of them says, "Old woman, I hold in my
      hand a bird. Tell

23   me whether it is living or dead."

24   She does not answer, and the question is repeated. "Is the bird I am holding
      living or

25   dead?"

26   Still she doesn't answer. She is blind and cannot see her visitors, let alone
      what is in their

27   hands. She does not know their color, gender or homeland. She only knows
      their motive.

28   The old woman's silence is so long, the young people have trouble holding
      their laughter.

29   Finally she speaks and her voice is soft but stern. "I don't know," she says. "I don't know

30   whether the bird you are holding is dead or alive, but what I do know is that it is in your

31   hands. It is in your hands."

32   Her answer can be taken to mean: if it is dead, you have either found it that way or you

33   have killed it. If is alive, you can still kill it. Whether it is to stay alive, it is your

34   decision. Whatever the case, it is your responsibility.

If we follow the rules to interpret the text, we see that one character is an old woman who is blind—she cannot see objects in front of her (line 24). Yet, she is called clairvoyant (19), so in at least one respect, she is able to see. She is also called "wise" (11). There are other characters in the text, namely, some young people who visit the old woman (18) and ask her a question that they believe she cannot answer, thereby hoping to prove that she is blind and ignorant—a "fraud" (18–23).

Following these rules to identify the characters and their actions prompts a question about the relation between the old woman and her visitors: Does the old woman fail to answer the young people's question because she cannot see whether the bird is alive or dead (26: "she is blind and cannot see her visitors") and so cannot answer the question? Or, does she say nothing because "She ... knows their motive" (27) and does not want to participate in a conversation with them? Is that why her silence is long (28)? If she does not want to participate in a conversation with them, why does she finally answer (29)?

Perplexity about the interpersonal relations between the old woman and the young people may arise in part from lack of familiarity with the setting in which the story takes place. Morrison says, "The honor she is paid and the awe in which she is held reach beyond her neighborhood to places far away; to the city where the intelligence of rural prophets is the source of much amusement" (14–17). Might the young people be from the city? Might they have come to amuse themselves at the old woman's expense, so that they approach her with disrespect—as she may suspect (27)?

In fact, the interpersonal relations between the old woman and the young people become more intriguing. The last lines of the text are as follows (lines 211–215, in appendix D):

It's quiet again when the children finish speaking, until the woman breaks into the silence.

"Finally," she says, "I trust you now. I trust you with the bird that is not in your hands because you have truly caught it. Look. How lovely it is, this thing we have done—together."

Seeing the opening of the speech and the closing, you might ask, Why does the old woman say that she trusts the young people in the end? What does she mean by, "I trust you with the bird that is not in your hands because you have truly caught it"?

The text was not one that I selected. I had been invited to lead a discussion with some seniors in an "underperforming" high school. The students, I was told, had never before participated in an interpretive discussion. My host selected the text, thinking that the students would find it of interest.

As it turned out, following the rules that govern the text, particularly those that present the relations between the characters, is not easy. For example, what does the word "it" refer to when the old woman says, "I know is that it is in your hands. It is in your hands" (31)? Does "it" refer to the bird? Or does the word "it" refer to the decision about whether to kill the bird? Perhaps it refers to neither.

Morrison's speech is an expository text. She begins by recounting a story, but since it is her Nobel speech, we know the story is recounted for some purpose. To address her purpose, she may need to address the point of ambiguity that I have just identified so that her view of the events in the story and the relation between the old woman and the young people becomes clear. So what does she take the old woman to mean in line 31?

Interestingly enough, the answer to that question is not clear. Morrison tells us, "Her answer can be taken to mean: if it is dead, you have either found it that way or you have killed it. If it is alive, you can still kill it" (32–33). Up to here, "it" seems to refer to the bird. However, things get messier. When Morrison continues to interpret the old woman's statement "Whether it is to stay alive, it is your decision" (33–34), the first "it" in the sentence refers to the bird, but the second "it" seems to refer to the decision about whether to kill the bird, assuming the bird is still alive. If the second "it" refers to the decision about whether to kill the bird, does the referent of "it" change in the sentence?

The ambiguity becomes even more perplexing with Morrison's interpretation of the old woman's meaning: "Whatever the case, it's your responsibility" (34). Does "Whatever the case" refer to the decision about whether to kill the bird, assuming that it is still alive? Or does "Whatever the case" refer to the bird and its condition—whether it is dead, alive, real or fictional, literally in the hand of the young people or not? Then again, does the phrase refer to the decision made by the young people to confront the old woman with the question about the bird? If the first "it" in line 31 refers to the bird rather than to the decision about whether to kill the bird, why does Morrison say, in interpreting the old woman: "If it [the bird] is dead, you have either found it that way … Whatever the case, it is your responsibility"? If the young people did find the bird dead, how could they be called responsible for its death?

In short, given Morrison's interpretation of the story about the old woman, another point of ambiguity arises: for what are the young people "responsible"? So far, the rules have been challenging. The relations between the young people and the old woman are ambiguous. In other words, thus far we are unable to identify the relations between the old woman and the young people in either the story or in Morrison's use of the story in her speech.

As it turns out, Morrison does not definitively resolve the point of ambiguity about the relation between the old woman and the young people. In fact, she keeps it very much alive as the speech continues. As we will see in chapter 6, the students participating in the discussion become intrigued with the ambiguity and eventually pursue its resolution through discussion. The text proves to be discussable. The students are able to identify a point of ambiguity that they care to resolve, and they make progress toward resolution in conversation with one another about the meaning of the text.

In identifying ambiguity, the leader of the expository text begins the same way that the leader of the fictional text begins, that is, by trying to follow the rules exhibited in the text and trying to identify the characters, their actions, the location of the actions, and the relations between the characters. In following the rules to identify these elements, the leader again encounters ambiguities.

CONCLUSION: SUITABILITY VERSUS DISCUSSABILITY

As argued earlier, ambiguity in a text is identified when a reader-observer follows the rules to interpret the text. By following those rules, the reader-observer can identify the characters, their actions, the location of the actions, the relations between the characters, and, indeed, the theme (ideas) with which the text is concerned. If in following the rules, the reader-observer encounters ambiguity (i.e., if the text or some aspect of it can be interpreted in more than one way), then the text may be suitable for interpretive discussion. Indeed, a necessary condition of a discussable text is that the leader can identify a point of ambiguity in it.[16]

However, all three texts discussed in this book may suffer from characteristics that could limit their suitability for discussion by groups and leaders. For example, when discussed at the Aurora School, Yevtushenko's *Schoolmaster* was studied as an English translation, not as the Russian language original. Arguably, the translation, itself an interpretation, conveys a different meaning from the original. Perhaps the meaning intended by the author is one to which those reading the work in English might not have access. Moreover, without factual knowledge of Russian schools of the twentieth century, a reader could misconstrue the second stanza of the poem and possibly the entire poem. Who is "Auntie Dear," anyway?

Likewise with "Rats," the text discussed by the seventh-grade science class, you might ask, How can an excerpt from a scientific work stand by itself as a discussable text? Might not its brevity mislead the reader? Shouldn't the participants read the entire book, *On Aggression*, from which the excerpt is taken, to grasp Lorenz's questions and insights regarding his empirical study of the species?

Finally, Toni Morrison's Nobel Prize lecture, although it is written and read in English, might arguably be too abstract and metaphorical for the discussants to grasp. As we will see, they struggled to understand the relations between the characters in the text, as well as the characters' motivations. How could these discussants have been expected to discover meaning in a text whose rules they could barely follow? And if they could not follow those rules, how could they be expected to grasp the purpose of this expository essay?

All of these are reasonable questions. Indeed, translations and excerpts can mislead the reader. What's more, meanings accessible to some readers-observers might be inaccessible to others because people lack experiences of various sorts and thus cannot discover meanings in the text.

At the same time, a text in translation, an abstract text abounding in metaphors, an excerpt from a longer work—all such texts may be discussable. As long as leaders and discussants are able to follow the semantic rules of the text well enough to discover points of ambiguity and textual evidence that addresses the ambiguities, the group may pursue conversation about its meaning.

More precisely, as long as leaders and discussants make progress identifying the characters, their actions, the location of the actions, the relations between the characters, and the themes pursued in the text, they will have access to at least some of the text's meaning. These are semantic rules—rules that govern meaning. In following the rules, they may discover points of ambiguity in the text. If the ambiguities are sufficiently complex, so that evidence may be found in various places to address them, then a discussion about the meaning of the text may take place and will focus on resolving the points of ambiguity.

Notice that a group might follow the rules but still not discover any points of ambiguity about meaning. In this case, the text is not discussable. The text may be too simple, in which case it provides sufficient evidence for the group to answer all the questions raised about the meaning of the text. Or it may be too vague to provide evidence that addresses the points of ambiguity that are identified. In either case, the text is not useful for an interpretive discussion.

Finally, a discussable text is not necessarily a suitable text. A text may prove highly ambiguous and offer evidence to support multiple resolutions but, at the same time, be poorly suited to the circumstances and purposes of the leader-teacher. People trying to learn Russian might make much more progress by reading *Schoolmaster* in the original language than in English, for example. Likewise, discussing excerpts abounding in ambiguity may be much less suitable than the study of an entire work or multiple works if the goal is to become knowledgeable about the perspective of a given author.

The suitability of the text depends upon many things, and teachers must consider the particular circumstances in order to make judgments about suitability. As mentioned in chapter 1, I selected *Schoolmaster* to discuss with the students at Aurora School because it was short (40 lines), I knew I had less than one hour for the conversation, and given its subject matter, I thought the discussants would find the poem of immediate interest. The situation seemed to render the poem suitable.

However, suitability is not the same as discussability, and our concern here is with the latter. As I have argued, whether or not a text is discussable is determined by perusing it—by following rules to identify the characters, their actions and motivations, the location of the actions, the relations between the characters, the themes or ideas within the text, and other characteristics of the text. In following the rules, the reader-observer may discover ambiguities about meaning, along with evidence to address the ambiguities.

How much ambiguity is needed to sustain a forty-five-minute discussion? How does a leader discover texts with sufficient ambiguity? We turn to those questions in chapter 3.

Preparing a Cluster
of Questions

How do you discover texts that have enough ambiguity to sustain discussion for forty-five minutes or more? Here's my acid test: if you can write a cluster of questions about the meaning of the text, then the text is discussable. If the discussants can follow rules that allow them to find meaning in the text, it will be discussable, and conversation about its meaning can be sustained for at least forty-five minutes.

As explained earlier, a cluster of questions is a set of interpretive questions about the meaning of the text. They may be resolved in more than one way, depending on textual evidence. The cluster includes a basic question, which expresses the leader's deepest point of doubt about the meaning of the text—the point of ambiguity that the leader most wishes to answer. For this basic question, the leader has written eight follow-up questions, which are included in the cluster. The follow-up questions, like the basic question, are interpretive: they ask about the meaning of the text and can be resolved in more than one way, in light of textual evidence. In addition, they point to passages in the text that, if interpreted in at least one way, suggest ways to resolve the basic question. Having written the cluster, the leader knows that there is at least one point of ambiguity that can be addressed by exploring at least eight places in the text. Exploring those passages will take at least forty-five minutes.

How does one go about generating a cluster of questions? Why is it necessary to do so before leading an interpretive discussion? To address these queries, I show how I prepared the cluster of questions for Yevtushenko's poem *Schoolmaster*. In the present chapter, we will become immersed in the experience of generating the cluster and thereby glean insight into the benefits of the activity.

Let me emphasize at the outset that developing a cluster of questions about the meaning of a text is not a mechanical process. Rather, it is an exciting and self-revelatory adventure. In preparing a cluster, you discover not only whether the text has enough ambiguity to sustain discussion, but also much about your own interests, beliefs, and values.

TURNING ON THE SPIGOT

To generate a cluster of questions, begin by writing down questions as you peruse the text. Any questions will do, as long as they are about things you wish to better understand. In writing down questions, don't worry about whether they will be answered as the study of the text goes on, whether they are interpretive, or whether you really want to answer them. Just write them down, number each question, and identify the page, line, or other specific place in the text to which the question refers.

For example, I wrote the following questions while reading the poem *Schoolmaster*:

1. Why does the schoolmaster have no name?
2. Why does the schoolmaster look out the window instead of teach arithmetic? (lines 3–4)
3. Why does he break his chalk? (5)
4. Who is saying or thinking line 7, "And he's forgotten the rules of long division," the schoolmaster or the students?
5. Does the schoolmaster have no name because he is every teacher or because he is an unremarkable teacher?
6. Who is the "We" in line 10, "We watch him with a different attention"?
7. Does the "We" in line 10 refer to the students in the class or a narrator and the reader?

8. Does the "we" in lines 14–16 refer to the students in the classroom since they do not know where the schoolmaster's wife has gone, but only know that she has gone away?

9. Do the students watch the schoolmaster (32) for the same reason they "watch him with a different attention" (10)—they are trying to understand the effects of aging, which is different from trying to understand the subject matter (arithmetic) that he teaches them?

10. Do the students note that the schoolmaster's clothes "are neither new nor in the fashion" (17) because they are now focused on the fact that he is getting older?

11. Do the students imagine that the schoolmaster is speaking to someone downstairs named "Auntie," (lines 22–27), whom they believe is there, rather than overhear a conversation? If so, is that why some words appear in single quotation marks?

12. If the students imagine the schoolmaster speaking, do they imagine him saying, "I'm getting old. You can't do much about getting old" (26–27) because they are thinking about him getting old?

13. If the students are trying to understand the effects of growing old at line 32, why do they say the schoolmaster's wife has gone (13–16) after they notice his mistake in long division (9)?

14. When the text says, "A little while longer will make him so white we shall not see him in the whitened trees" (39–40), does it mean that the schoolmaster will be forgotten as an individual? Is that why he is given no name?

I wrote more questions, but haven't included them here. All of the questions in the preceding list arise from the attempt to follow the rules governing the text—rules about who the characters are, what they do, the locations of the actions, the relations between the characters, the themes or ideas with which the text is concerned, and other characteristics of the text. As we look at the questions, do we see the deepest point of doubt emerging—the question that the leader wishes most to resolve?

PERUSING THE WRITTEN QUESTIONS TO FIND A POINT OF GENUINE DOUBT

Writing questions as you read is helpful for at least three reasons. First, the written list captures ideas that might otherwise escape into nothingness. If you simply generate questions while perusing the text and write them all down without judging them good or bad, right or wrong, interesting or not interesting, and so on, there are bound to be some questions of interest among those on the list. By writing questions, you capture data about your own interests with respect to the text, and those data are valuable—indeed, invaluable.

Second, writing questions is like turning on the spigot. Once the tap is opened, the questions will continue to flow. In writing the first question, you give yourself permission to write down more questions as they occur while you read the text, and so the questions begin to come. But they have to be written down as they arise. And you have to put aside judgment while writing the questions, lest the spigot get turned off.

Third, the list of questions teaches you about your interests. In order to write a cluster of questions, you need to discover the deepest point of doubt—the question you wish most to resolve about the meaning of the text. The discovery is facilitated by generating and then perusing all the questions you have written. Not all will appear interesting, but some will, or to put it a bit differently, some questions will help you move toward the question you wish most to resolve.

So, what do the written questions show about the leader's deepest point of doubt? Let's take a look.

To begin to study the questions, we must first ask, Are all of the questions on the list interpretive? That is, can they be resolved in more than one way on the basis of textual evidence? Or, are some of the questions factual—questions that can be resolved definitively by pointing to a particular place in the text. Factual questions have answers that will probably not be disputed, so while they might have an important role in an actual discussion, they are set aside when preparing the cluster questions.[1] Nor will the leader include evaluative questions in the cluster—those that ask for judgment about whether what the text says is right, wrong, correct, informative, or irrelevant.[2] Because all of the questions on the preceding list look to be interpretive, we consider each in trying to identify the leader's deepest point of doubt. (For a discussion of factual, evaluative, and interpretive questions, please see appendix E.)

Questions 1, 5, and 14 concern why the schoolmaster is given no name. Questions 6, 7, and 8 ask about the referent for the word "we" in particular lines of the poem. Questions 9, 10, 12, and 13 wonder what the students are thinking at line 32 as they watch their teacher. When several questions pertain to an issue, this suggests that the leader-writer has (or had) interest in the issue. So, within the entire list of questions, three issues seem to be of greatest concern. Further evidence of interest in the three issues is that the leader suggested ideas about answers to them as the reading of the text and the writing of the questions progressed.

Take question 1, "Why does the schoolmaster have no name?" It is phrased as an *open* question, meaning that no idea about its resolution is offered. Question 5, on the other hand, is phrased as an *issue* question, that is, it offers two possible, perhaps mutually exclusive resolutions: "Does the schoolmaster have no name because he is every teacher or because he is an unremarkable teacher?" Question 14 is phrased as a *single-possibility* question, meaning it offers one idea about the answer—that in the speaker's mind, the schoolmaster will blend in with other teachers and will be forgotten as an individual. Furthermore, it quotes a passage from the text to support the idea. The emergence of several possible answers to the question and the leader's appeals to textual evidence to evaluate one possibility suggest that interest in the question of why the schoolmaster has no name is furthered by continued study of the text.

Notice that although questions 6, 7, and 8 ask about the referent for the term "we," the number of other questions suggests that the leader loses interest in that issue, as later questions are unrelated to these three. And why does the leader lose interest? Did the identity of "we" turn out to be a factual question that can be resolved definitively by pointing to a particular passage? Question 6 ("Who is the 'We' in line 10, 'We watch him with a different attention'?") is phrased as an open question: no ideas about the answer are suggested.[3] Question 7 suggests two possible resolutions—that "we" refers to the students in the schoolteacher's class or the narrator plus the reader. In question 7, the suggested resolutions do not point to evidence that supports them. However, question 8 looks at lines in the text and asks, "Does the 'we' in lines 14–16 refer to students in the classroom since they do not know where the schoolmaster's wife has gone, but only that she has gone away?"

The question asks whether these lines are spoken by young students who are not privy to the details of the wife's departure. A narrator and reader certainly could have access to such details. Hence, the "we" refers to the students, or so the leader's reasoning seems to go.

In short, although the leader does not fully interpret lines 14–16 and argue that these lines seem to be spoken by elementary-school-age children in the schoolmaster's classroom, she seems to take the lines as sufficient to establish the referent for "we" in the poem. Since she wrote no further questions about that issue, she seems to have resolved it to her satisfaction, although one might challenge her resolution.[4] Indeed, subsequent questions on the list (i.e., questions 9 through 13) presuppose this resolution—that the "we" refers to the students.

By contrast, the question of what the students ponder as they watch their teacher in line 32 seems to become more pressing as the leader continues to study the text. Question 9 takes up the issue. It draws attention to line 10—"We watch him with a different attention." What is "different" about that attention? the leader asks. At line 32, "we" are watching the schoolmaster again, but are "we" watching him for the same reason as at line 10? Question 9 suggests that in line 32, "we" are thinking about the effects of aging. Might their preoccupation at line 10 be the same, so that the "difference" referred to in line 10 is that they are pondering the effects of aging rather than arithmetic? In question 10, textual evidence for the effects-of-aging resolution is given in line 17, where the students observe that the teacher's clothes are neither new nor fashionable.

In question 12, there is more evidence that the students may be pondering the effects of growing older. Here, the leader looks at lines 26–27 and raises the possibility that if the students imagine their teacher saying, "I'm getting old. You can't do much about getting old," it is because they themselves are thinking about the consequences of his growing older.

However, in question 13, the leader focuses on some apparently contradictory evidence: if the students are watching the schoolmaster and trying to understand the effects of aging, then why do they take four lines (13–16) to say that his wife is gone? Could they be pondering the effects of losing one's wife, rather than the effects of aging?

In the list of questions, there seem to be two candidates for the leader's deepest point of doubt—the question she wishes most to resolve about the meaning of the text. First, why does the schoolmaster have no name in the poem? (Questions 1,5, and 14 relate to the issue). And second, what do the students ponder as they watch their teacher? (Questions 9 through 13 relate to the issue.) About which issue does the leader have greater concern, and how does she decide?

The decision depends not only on the strength of the felt concern but also on whether the leader can write eight follow-up questions about the issue. In the section that follows, we will see why writing eight follow-up questions is the acid test and why only one of the two candidates for the leader's deepest point of doubt passes the test.

USING THE DEEPEST POINT OF DOUBT TO DEVELOP A CLUSTER OF QUESTIONS

The candidate for the deepest point of doubt becomes the basic question of the cluster of questions.[5] The basic question is the one that the entire cluster aims to resolve. The cluster consists of the basic question and eight follow-up questions, all of which are interpretive. The follow-up questions each point to a place in the text that, if interpreted in at least one way, suggests an idea about the resolution of the basic question.

Writing follow-up questions is important for at least three reasons. First, you want to see if there are eight places in the text that, if interpreted in at least one way, suggest a way to resolve the basic question. Each follow-up question will identify such a place, interpret it, and ask a question about its meaning in relation to that deepest point of doubt. Having written eight such questions, a leader is confident that there is sufficient textual evidence to sustain a forty-five-minute discussion about the answer to the basic question.[6]

Second, in writing the follow-up questions, you are bound to clarify the basic question—to revise and express your deepest point of doubt with increasing precision and, in so doing, say more clearly what you care to resolve. For example, if in writing follow-up questions, a leader discovers that most of the evidence seems to support one or two resolutions of the basic question, as actually happened in my preparation for the discussion of *Schoolmaster*, the leader would change the basic question to incorporate those ideas about resolution.

Third, writing follow-up questions helps you clarify your interpretation of the text. Why? In writing each question, you identify a passage that has implication for resolving the basic question. You try to say in your own words what the passage says, and then draw the implication for the resolution. This step requires you to examine the text more closely and may clarify your understanding.

In the *Schoolmaster* example, we have two candidates for the leader's deepest point of doubt and thus two candidates for the basic question of the cluster. Are they equally viable? That is, could a leader write eight follow-up questions about each one?

As it happened, the leader came up with these follow-up questions for the first basic question candidate ("According to the text, why does the schoolmaster have no name?"):

1. Does the schoolmaster have no name because he is every teacher or because he is an unremarkable teacher?
2. When the text says, "A little longer will make him so white we shall not see him in the whitened trees" (39–40), does it mean that the schoolmaster will be forgotten as an individual?
3. If the schoolmaster has no name because the poet is saying he will be forgotten as an individual, then why is the poem written about him?

Here, the list of follow-up questions stops. The leader was unable to write more questions pointing to passages in the text that suggested ideas about why the schoolmaster has no name in the poem. That is not to say that another leader might not have made more progress. But given that this leader could write only three follow-up questions, she had to abandon the proposed basic question candidate, having insufficient evidence that it could sustain a forty-five minute discussion.

Fortunately, she was more successful with the second candidate for the deepest point of doubt ("What do the students ponder as they watch their teacher?") and did generate eight follow-up questions. Some of these appeared on the original list, some are modified, and some are completely new questions.

Here are the follow-up questions for the second basic question candidate ("What do the students ponder as they watch their teacher?"):

1. Do the students watch the schoolmaster (32) because they feel sorry for him? If they feel sorry for him, is it because his wife has gone away (13–16) or because he is getting old?

2. Do the students watch the schoolmaster (32) for the same reason they "watch him with a different attention" (10)—they are trying to understand the effects of aging, which is different from trying to understand the arithmetic he usually teaches?

3. Do the students watch the schoolmaster (32) because they are feeling sad that their teacher is aging and will leave them? Is this what they realize when they say that they are "needing no one to hint to [them]" (11) about why the schoolmaster has made a mistake on the blackboard?

4. Do the students note that the schoolmaster wears the same unfashionable suit (17–19) because this tells them he is aging or because this tells them he is unhappy that his wife has gone away?

5. Do the students imagine the schoolmaster's words and actions in the cloakroom (21–28)? If so, do they do so because they are reflecting on the consequences of aging or the consequences of losing one's wife?

6. Do the students watch the schoolmaster (32) for the same reason he watches the trees (4)? Are both students and teacher trying to understand what happens to people when they get old, or are they trying to understand what happens to people when they lose someone they love?

7. Do the students notice that the schoolmaster has a bent back (33) because they are pondering the effects of aging or the effects of losing one's wife? If the former, does the narrator correct himself and say the schoolmaster is "worn out" (35) because he concludes the clumsy walking comes from aging?

8. In saying, "A little longer will make him so white we shall not see him in the whitened trees" (39–40), do the students conclude that their memory of the teacher will disappear as they age?

Once eight follow-up questions have been written, the next step in preparing the cluster is to ask, Are they good questions? That is, do they demonstrate that the leader has identified a clear point of ambiguity about the meaning of the text? In the next section, we use several criteria to evaluate the initial cluster of questions.

EVALUATING THE CLUSTER OF QUESTIONS

In *Learning to Teach Through Discussion: The Art of Turning the Soul*, I present the following criteria with which to evaluate a cluster of questions.[7] These criteria have been developed though my experience as a discussion leader and a teacher educator. There are eight criteria that a well-formed cluster of questions needs to meet:

1. The cluster consists of a basic question and at least eight follow-up questions.
2. All the questions in the cluster—the basic question and follow-up questions—are interpretive questions, meaning that they can be resolved in at least two ways, given textual evidence.
3. All the questions are clear. They are free of technical terms—terms that could have more than one meaning and the intended meaning is unclear. They are they free of vague phrases.
4. The follow-up questions quote or otherwise identify a particular passage in the text. They interpret the quoted passage fully. That is, they say, in the writer's own words, no more and no less than what the passage says. The point of reference (page, line, or other location) is indicated precisely.
5. The basic question expresses the deepest point of doubt—the question that the leader wishes most to resolve.[8]
6. All questions in the cluster follow up the basic question. That is, resolving each question in at least one way suggests an idea about resolution of the basic question.
7. The basic question is in the proper form. If the answers to the follow-up questions seem to support two resolutions of the basic question, the two resolutions are expressed in the question. If most of the answers to the follow-up questions support one resolution, then the basic question should suggest that resolution. If the answers to the follow-up questions suggest three or more resolutions of the basic question, then it should be stated in open form (i.e., offer no possible resolution) and the possibilities should be suggested by the follow-up questions. The form of the basic question should indicate the questioner's best guess about the resolution.
8. All questions in the cluster explore the leader's deepest point of doubt about the meaning of the text in as few words as possible: the basic question is clear and posed in as few words as possible; the follow-up questions quote just enough text to provide evidence for the suggested interpretation; the quoted words are interpreted fully but in as few words as possible.

If we apply the preceding criteria to the original cluster, we see that it has short-comings.[9] The application of the criteria allows us to clarify the cluster because it directs us to make certain modifications in the questions. Table 3-1 shows which criteria each question fails to meet.

Looking at the cluster overall, we see that six of the eight follow-up questions fail to meet criterion 4: they fail to either cite particular passages or interpret them fully. Furthermore, six of the eight follow-up questions fail to meet criterion 6: they fail to relate the interpretation of the quoted words to resolution of the basic question.

Question 1 does not quote and interpret a particular passage and does not suggest a resolution of the basic question in light of an interpretation. Questions 3, 4, 5, and 8 all quote or refer to specific lines. However, these questions do not present full interpretations of the quoted words. They fail at trying to say no more and no less than what the quoted words say and at relating the interpretation to the resolution of the basic question. Question 7 begins to interpret line 35, but more work needs to be done.

Two of the four follow-up questions and the basic question fail to meet criterion 3: the point of doubt is not clear. The basic question does not identify the place or places in the text where the reader would be unclear about the thinking of the students. And is question 2 concerned with whether the students watch the school-master for the same reason in lines 10 and 32? Or is it concerned with whether they are trying to understand the effects his growing older? Does question 6 ask whether the students in line 32 and the schoolmaster in line 4 think about the same thing when they watch the trees? Or is it about what each is thinking?

Finally, even though the basic question is in open form, all of the follow-up questions suggest one of two resolutions. Therefore the basic question fails to meet criterion 7: it should be stated in issue form.[10] The consequence of these shortcomings is that as the cluster stands, it does not make much progress toward resolving the basic question.

Because our evaluation of the cluster identifies specific shortcomings, we may revise the questions to address these shortcomings (table 3-2). Consider the revised questions with respect to the criteria that were presented above. No doubt, the questions could be further clarified. At the same time, they seem to be clearer now than they were. They also make more progress toward the resolution of the deepest point of doubt, which is now more clearly stated by the basic question.

TABLE 3-1 **The cluster of suggested questions for** *Schoolmaster* **and their drawbacks**

Question	Criteria failed*
Basic question: What do the students ponder as they watch their teacher?	7, 3
1. Do the students watch the schoolmaster (32) because they feel sorry for him? If they feel sorry for him, is it because his wife has gone away (13–16) or because he is getting old?	4, 6
2. Do the students watch the schoolmaster (32) for the same reason they "watch him with a different attention" (10)—they are trying to understand the effects of his wife's absence, which is different from trying to understand the arithmetic he usually teaches?	3
3. Do the students watch the schoolmaster in silence (32) because they are feeling sad that their teacher is aging and will leave them? Is this what they realize when they say that they are needing no one to hint to [them] about why the schoolmaster has made a mistake on the blackboard (11)?	4, 6
4. Do the students note that the schoolmaster wears the same unfashionable suit (17–19) because this tells them he is aging or because this tells them he is unhappy that his wife has gone away?	4, 6
5. Do the students imagine the schoolmaster's words and actions in the cloakroom (21–28)? If so, do they do so because they are reflecting on the consequences of his aging or the consequences of his losing his wife?	4, 6
6. Do the students watch the schoolmaster (32) for the same reason he watches the trees (4)? Are both students and the schoolmaster trying to understand what happens to people when they get old, or are they trying to understand what happens to people when they lose someone they love?	3
7. Do the students notice that the schoolmaster has a bent back (33) because they are pondering the effects of aging or the effects of losing one's wife? If the former, does the narrator correct himself and say the schoolmaster is "worn out" (35) because he concludes that the clumsy walking comes from aging?	4, 6
8. In saying, "A little longer will make him so white we shall not see him in the whitened trees" (39–40), do the students conclude that their memory of the teacher will disappear as they age?	4, 6

*See text for details of numbered criteria.

TABLE 3-2 **Revised cluster of questions for** *Schoolmaster*

Original	Revised
Basic question: What do the students ponder as they watch their teacher?	Do the students watch the schoolmaster in silence (32) because they are trying to understand the effects of growing old or the effects of his wife's absence?*

The revised basic question specifies a point of reference (line 32), to which the point of doubt refers (criterion 3). Originally, it was in open form, although many of the follow-up questions suggested one of two resolutions. The newly revised basic question is in issue form and identifies the two possibilities (criterion 7).

1. Do the students watch the schoolmaster (32) because they feel sorry for him? If they feel sorry for him, is it because his wife has gone away (13–16) or because he is getting old?	When the students say, "The schoolmaster's wife has gone away" (13), does it mean they know that the schoolmaster's wife is no longer living with him? If so, do they watch the schoolmaster in silence (32) because they are trying to understand the effects of his wife's absence?

The original question did not quote or interpret a specific passage (criterion 4) and did not work toward resolving the basic question (criterion 6). The newly revised question does both.

2. Do the students watch the schoolmaster (32) for the same reason they "watch him with a different attention" (10)—they are trying to understand the effects of his wife's absence, which is different from trying to understand the arithmetic he usually teaches?	When the students say," We watch him with a different attention" (10), do they mean that since he has made a mistake in arithmetic (9), they are no longer thinking about arithmetic but about why he made the error? If so, do they then ponder the wife's absence in lines 13–16, and possibly in line 32, in an effort to understand why the teacher made a mistake? (Note that by interpreting line 10 fully, the leader got a different idea about the implication of the quoted words for the resolution of the basic question.)

The point of doubt in the original question was unclear (criterion 3). Were the students watching the schoolmaster for the same reason in both line 10 and line 32, or were they trying to understand the effects of his wife's absence? The newly revised question clarifies the point of doubt.

(continued)

TABLE 3-2 *continued* **Revised cluster of questions for** *Schoolmaster*

Original	Revised
3. Do the students watch the schoolmaster in silence (32) because they are feeling sad that their teacher is aging and will leave them? Is this what they realize when they say that they are "needing no one to hint to [them]" about why the school-master has made a mistake on the blackboard (11)?	When the students say that they are "needing no one to hint to [them]" (11), do they mean that they don't need other people to explain to them why their teacher has made a mistake, since they can figure it out for themselves? If they ponder the wife's absence in lines 13–16 to figure out why the teacher made the mistake, have they changed their minds about the reason by the time they watch him at line 32, as they remark that he looks "worn out" (35)?

The original question did not attempt to interpret the quoted text (criterion 4), and did not work toward resolving the basic question (criterion 6). The newly revised question does both.

Original	Revised
4. Do the students note that the schoolmaster wears the same unfashionable suit (17–19) because this tells them he is aging or because this tells them he is unhappy that his wife has gone away?	When the students say, "His clothes are neither new nor in the fashion; wearing the suit which he always wears" (17–18), does it mean that the schoolmaster's clothes are old, look out of date, and that he wears the same clothes to school every day? If so, are the students beginning to think about the effects of growing old—a topic they continue to ponder in line 32?

The original question did not quote or interpret specific text (criterion 4) and did not work toward resolving the basic question (criterion 6). The newly revised question does both.

Original	Revised
5. Do the students imagine the schoolmaster's words and actions in the cloakroom (21–28)? If so, do they do so because they are reflecting on the consequences of his aging or the consequences of his losing his wife?	When the students imagine the schoolmaster saying, 'I'm getting old … You can't do much about getting old' (25–27), do they mean that the teacher is aware of his advancing age and believes he has no control over it? If so, do the students attribute these words to their teacher because they think his aging may have caused him to err at the blackboard and he knows it?

The original question did not quote or interpret a specific passage (criterion 4) and did not work toward resolving the basic question (criterion 6). The revised question does both.

(continued)

TABLE 3-2 *continued* **Revised cluster of questions for** *Schoolmaster*

Original	Revised
6. Do the students watch the schoolmaster (32) for the same reason he watches the trees (4)? Are both students and the schoolmaster trying to understand what happens to people when they get old, or are they trying to understand what happens to people when they lose someone they love?	When the text says, "The master looks out … at the trees … breaking his chalk in one hand" (2–5), does it mean that the teacher stares at the trees and breaks chalk in his hand because he realizes his arithmetical error and feels impatient with himself for making it? If so, do the students watch the schoolmaster in silence at line 32 because they are pondering the effects of aging, and having observed their teacher's arithmetical error, wonder whether aging has lessened his competence?

The point of doubt in the original question was unclear (criterion 3): Were the students watching the schoolmaster for the same reason that he watches the trees? Or what were the students (32) and schoolmaster (4) thinking about? The newly revised question clarifies the point of doubt.

7. Do the students notice that the schoolmaster has a bent back (33) because they are pondering the effects of aging or the effects of losing one's wife? If the former, does the narrator correct himself and say the schoolmaster is "worn out" (35) because he concludes that the clumsy walking comes from aging?	When the text says, "He moves without defenses, clumsily, worn out I ought to have said, clumsily" (34–35), does it mean that the speaker is a student presenting the students' view and sees the schoolmaster's awkward movements as a consequence of aging? Is that why the words "worn out" are added to the description of the teacher? If so, does it mean that the students look in silence at the schoolmaster in line 32 because they see that aging makes one very tired?

The original question makes some attempt to interpret the text, but it quotes so few words that the understanding of meaning is limited (criterion 4). Further, the original question does not work toward resolving the basic question (criterion 6). The newly revised question quotes more, interprets the text more fully, and tries to resolve the basic question.

(continued)

TABLE 3-2 *continued*   Revised cluster of questions for *Schoolmaster*

Original	Revised
8. In saying, "A little longer will make him so white we shall not see him in the whitened trees" (39–40), do the students conclude that their memory of the teacher will disappear as they age?	In saying, "A little longer will make him so white we shall not see him in the whitened trees," (39–40), do the students mean that with more time, the snow will make the schoolmaster so white that they will no longer recognize his shape among the white trees? If so, does it mean that they are looking at him in silence at line 32 because they believe that as they age, they will no longer remember him clearly?

The original question did not attempt to interpret the quoted text (criterion 4) and did not work toward resolving the basic question (criterion 6). The newly revised question does both.

*Unlike the earlier version of the basic question offered in chapter 1, one of the possible resolutions has been rephrased to express the deepest point of doubt more precisely: "the effects of losing one's wife" has become "the effects of his wife's absence."

CONCLUSION

Developing a cluster of questions about the meaning of the text takes time. Nevertheless, revising the questions according to the eight criteria helps to clarify the basic question—the question that the leader wishes most to resolve. It also tests the depth of the ambiguity, for the follow-up questions demonstrate that if interpreted in at least one way, at least eight places in the text suggest ideas about the resolution of the basic question. The ability to write the cluster persuades the leader that a text can sustain at least forty-five minutes of discussion. A good cluster points out at least one point of ambiguity whose resolution may be explored through the study of eight (or more) locations in the text. Furthermore, revision of the questions—and it often takes four or five rounds of revision before the cluster of questions meets all eight criteria—requires repeated examination of the text. The more you reflect on the text, the clearer your interpretation and the greater your desire to discuss the text with others to further understand the work.

Until now, we have focused on the leader's preparation for discussion. We have seen that in preparing the cluster of questions, a leader tries to clarify the question he or she wishes most to resolve about the meaning of the text. You might ask, What of the students? Suppose they are interested in a different question? And will the leader ask all those follow-up questions that he or she has worked so hard to develop? Suppose the students interpret the text in ways the leader never imagined?

These and more questions are addressed in part 2, "Leading the Discussion." In chapters 4, 5, and 6, we use excerpts from actual interpretive discussions to consider these questions.

PART TWO

Leading the Discussion

A Discussion of Yevgeny Yevtushenko's *Schoolmaster*

WE COME NOW to the topic of discussion leading itself. In order to explore it, chapters 4, 5, and 6 each reflect upon a discussion that took place in a classroom setting. These conversations about three different kinds of texts—*Schoolmaster*, by Yevtushenko; "Rats," taken from *On Aggression*, by Konrad Lorenz; and the Nobel Laureate speech delivered by Toni Morrison in 1993—were introduced in the introduction, chapter 1, and chapter 2. In the present chapter, as well as chapters 5 and 6, we look at excerpts from these discussions.

One focus in chapter 4 is on the leader of the discussions. What does the leader do to help the discussants clarify questions they want to answer and progress toward resolution? As indicated throughout the book, the leader follows discussion-leading patterns—patterns requiring habits of mind that are cultivated as the patterns are followed.[1]

A second focus is on the discussants themselves. How do they respond to patterns initiated by the leader? They learn to follow the patterns and respond appropriately, initiating the patterns and acquiring the skills and habits of mind needed for effective participation in interpretive discussion.

SETTING UP THE DISCUSSION

The discussion of *Schoolmaster* took place in the Aurora School, a suburban, independent preK–12 school. I was invited to lead a discussion with a group of honors English sophomores who were students of a Northwestern alumna, Ms. Bright. She had been teaching at Aurora School for six years and had engaged her students in interpretive discussions. Hence, the pedagogical approach was not entirely new to them.

Ms. Bright knew that an interpretive discussion group of high school students should have between ten and fifteen participants—the ideal size if everyone is going to speak at least three times in the course of a forty-five-minute discussion.[2] If the group becomes larger than fifteen or sixteen, then it becomes difficult to accomplish what I call *equal air time*—every participant speaking at least three times and for about the same amount of time.[3] In general, equal airtime makes it possible for each person in the discussion to develop the speaking and listening skills required for successful discussion participation.

As is ideal, Ms. Bright had arranged the chairs in her classroom to form a circle so that all the participants could see one another and the leader, who would sit in the circle with the others. The circular seating arrangement helps create a sense of equity within the group, as no one is located in front of or above the others. The sense of equity is furthered by the assumption that all participants, including the leader, come together seeking to understand the meaning of some text and that all have access to it. Often, the leader is more familiar with it than others in the group, having prepared a cluster of questions about its meaning.

As described in chapter 1, the leader began the discussion of *Schoolmaster* by learning the participants' names. Names can be learned quickly by playing the name game, which goes like this: after soliciting the participants' approval for the practice of addressing one another by first names, the leader asks the participant to her right to state his or her first name.[4] The next discussant to the right repeats the first speaker's name and adds his or hers to the list. The discussants proceed in like fashion, always repeating the names in order and adding their own name to the end of the list. The last discussant—the one seated to the left of the leader—recites all the preceding names, adding his or her name to the end of the list. The leader repeats all the names in order—forward at least, and backward in addition, if desired. And of course, the leader adds his or her own name to the end of the list. Sound like a formidable task? Under normal circumstances, it is not.[5] With groups of ten to fifteen and all that repetition, people come to associate the name with the face. Hence, it is imperative that everyone be able to see everyone else—another advantage of the circular seating arrangement. All participants usually succeed in reciting the list of names, as they usually pay close attention while each speaker does so.

Learning the names of the participants before the discussion begins has many benefits and is worth the few minutes it takes. First, it sends the message that the leader wants to know the names, not simply read them off a card as a matter of momentary convenience. Second, it helps all the participants know each other's names, which often they do not, even in classrooms where they have been together for days or weeks. Third, it allows the leader to focus upon what people are saying rather than trying to remember names as the discussion proceeds.[6] Finally, the name game played with focus immediately binds the leader and participants together as a community of seekers.

THE DISCUSSION PROPER

Our study focuses on the first twenty-five minutes of the *Schoolmaster* discussion. Here the shared point of doubt—a question that more than one discussant works to address—begins to form. We also see patterns that the leader follows to help the discussants clarify their questions, identify the shared point of doubt, and pursue resolution. Although at first the discussion seems to flounder, under the leader's guidance the discussants begin to develop appropriate listening patterns and convincing arguments.

At the request of the group, the discussion began with the leader's prepared basic question: "Do the students watch schoolmaster in silence at line 32 because they are trying to understand the effects of growing old or because they are trying to understand the effects of losing one's wife?"

As described earlier, the leader followed certain discussion-leading patterns. She posed a basic question developed previously, which immediately gave the group a possible point of focus. The question was directed at a particular participant and asked directly about the meaning of a line in the text. It also suggested interpretations for the participants to consider. As the discussion progressed, the leader followed additional patterns—asking for textual evidence and repeating back what she understood the discussant to mean.

Let's pick up where we left things with Michael in chapter 1. Instead of addressing the leader's question, Michael has shifted to the more general issue of what the poem is about. And when he says, "He [the schoolmaster] makes a mistake on the blackboard seemingly because his wife has left," Michael seems to shift the question again, now trying to explain why the schoolmaster made the mistake on the blackboard (line 9). So what is the question that Michael most wishes to resolve? If clarified, it might be one that others would care to address as well. The leader proceeds as follows:

> **SHG:** Okay, Michael, that's great. Could you tell us ... Let's have some line numbers here. Just so we can follow exactly what you're saying. So you had said in this first stanza, you mentioned several places where he seems to be getting old. That was the first idea that you had, right?
>
> **MICHAEL:** Right, correct.
>
> **SHG:** He's "declining," is your word.
>
> **MICHAEL:** Right.
>
> **SHG:** So what line numbers tell you that?
>
> **MICHAEL:** Lines 5 through 9.

Here, to confirm her understanding of Michael's intended meaning, the leader repeats back something she believes Michael has said: "He [the schoolmaster] seems to be getting old. That was the first idea you had, right?" Also: "He's 'declining' is your word." In each case, Michael agrees that he has been correctly understood.

The leader also asks Michael to provide textual evidence for claims that he makes. If he believes that the schoolmaster is getting old or "declining" in the poem, what lines in the poem lead him to draw that inference?

Since Michael supplies line numbers that, he says, contain evidence for his inference, the leader asks him to read the evidence he has identified and to explain how it justifies his claim, as he does not do so on his own initiative:

> **SHG:** Okay, so why don't you read those lines aloud, and let's see your argument there.

MICHAEL [reading]: "Breaking his chalk slowly in one hand. And it's only the rules of long division. And he's forgotten the rules of long division. Imagine not remembering long division! A mistake on the blackboard, a mistake." It seems as though [these lines have] truly captivated the persona of the schoolmaster who we're introduced to first who [becomes] almost the dominant [character] of the poem. [He] is doing something new, which is making a mistake, forgetting the rules of long division.

SHG: So why is he making a mistake?

Now, in the context of an interpretive discussion, an argument that defends a claim well has three parts. First, it cites and reads the textual evidence that supports the claim. Second, it interprets the evidence, that is, it tries to say what the quoted words seem to mean. Third, it explains why the quoted words, interpreted as they have been, support the claim (see the sidebar "Using Text to Support a Claim").[7]

USING TEXT TO SUPPORT A CLAIM

1. Cite the textual evidence.
2. Interpret the evidence (say what the quoted words mean).
3. Explain why the evidence, if interpreted correctly, supports the claim.

When Michael says that the schoolmaster is "doing something new … making a mistake, forgetting the rules of long division," he may be interpreting the lines to mean that the teacher has made an error, something the man has not done before, because he has forgotten how to divide numbers. Michael may infer that the error is due to aging. But is that his reasoning? It is hard to follow, so the leader asks him to clarify his argument: "So why is he making a mistake"? Asking directly about the meaning of something a discussant has said is another discussion-leading pattern that leaders often follow. Michael responds:

MICHAEL: Well, if you compare these five lines in the second stanza to the lines … excuse me … to the last four lines of [the first] stanza, lines 13 to 16, it seems as though he is almost distracted by the fact that his wife has gone away. I saw a parallel … Long division could be representing the division of the wife and the schoolmaster.

SHG: Uh-huh.

Here, Michael does two things that challenge an attempt to follow his argument. First, he does not fully interpret lines 5–9 and explain why they imply that the schoolmaster erred because he is getting old ("declining"). Instead, Michael says, "if you compare these five lines with … lines 13 to 16, it seems as though he is almost distracted by the fact that his wife has gone away."

Second, when Michael brings up lines 13–16, he does not interpret them but instead uses them as evidence to answer the leader's question, "So why is he [the schoolmaster] making a mistake?" Michael does not seem to understand that she is asking, How do you interpret lines 5–9 so as to explain why the schoolmaster errs?

The student continues:

MICHAEL: So I sort of … I set those two against each other and I see that they're sort of equal. That the schoolmaster's wife has gone away is the same in the sense as the schoolmaster forgetting long division.

Here, Michael seems to return to the idea of the parallel that he sees. He asserts that the departure of the schoolmaster's wife is like the departure of the rules of long division from the schoolmaster's mind. But even if he is right, how does the presence of the parallel address the question of why the schoolmaster makes a mistake with long division on the blackboard? That is the question he has raised and seems concerned with answering.

It may be that Michael has studied poetry as a genre and has learned that the use of language therein can follow particular rules unique to it.[8] Indeed, he seems to interpret the poem by trying to follow rules that obtain in poetry as a genre, which may lead him to look for and identify parallels and reversals between the events. But again, even if the departure of the wife is like forgetting the rules of long division, how does that observation help Michael answer the question of why the schoolmaster makes a mistake with long division on the blackboard?

In what follows, the leader tries to help Michael make arguments to support his claims:

SHG: Well, it is … interesting, because I've heard two ideas … One is that he [the schoolmaster] forgets the long division because he's distracted, okay, which we see in lines 5 to 9 … or perhaps because he's distracted by the wife's having gone away, which we see in lines 13 to 16, right? We didn't read those aloud, but that's what you're seeing in lines 13 to 16, so where the schoolmaster's wife has gone away: "We do not know where she has gone to, we do not know why she has gone, what we know is his wife has gone away." So part of what I heard you say was, he's forgetting the rules of long division because he's distracted by the departure of his wife.

MICHAEL: Right.

Because Michael did not follow the practice of reading lines 13–16, then interpreting them, and then explaining why they are evidence that the schoolmaster made a mistake because he was distracted by the wife's departure, the leader takes the first step and reads those lines. Listening, Michael agrees that yes, he has maintained that the schoolmaster may have forgotten the rules of long division because his wife's departure has shifted his focus. So together, leader and participant have started to defend the claim that the schoolmaster errs because his wife has left him. The discussion continues:

SHG: But earlier I heard you say … that you saw this schoolmaster as a case of somebody in decline. Those were the words I believe you used, right? He was getting older, okay … Is there evidence in the second stanza that he's declining, as you put it?

The leader's preceding comments reveal three habits of mind, or three ways of directing attention. Experienced leaders exercise these habits repeatedly (see the sidebar "The Discussion Leader's Habits of Mind").

THE DISCUSSION LEADER'S HABITS OF MIND

- Listen to grasp the speaker's intended meaning.
- Listen to identify the speaker's question and ideas about resolution.
- Listen to determine the strength of the speaker's argument for resolving the question.

First, she listens carefully to Michael to understand what he intends to say, and to remember it. She says that she has heard "two ideas … One is that [the schoolmaster] forgets the long division because he is distracted … by the wife's having gone away" and adds, "But earlier I heard you say … that you saw the schoolmaster as a case of somebody in decline." The leader repeats the two claims that she has heard Michael make and, in so doing, places them before the speaker and others in the group for evaluation. Has she understood Michael's intended meaning?

Second, when she says, "So part of what I heard you say was, he's forgetting the rules of long division because he's distracted by the departure of his wife," she is listening to Michael to identify the question he wants to answer and what he says in response to it. She repeats back ideas she has heard him express and in relation to the question that seems to concern him: why the schoolmaster makes a mistake at the blackboard when doing long division.

Third, the leader listens to the discussant and asks herself, Is his argument convincing? Evidently, she thinks it is not, which may be why she initiates patterns aimed at helping him strengthen it. These include focusing his attention on particular lines that he has mentioned and asking him to read the lines and explain his argument, which would involve interpreting the quoted lines fully and explaining why they support his claims.

Effective discussion leaders exercise these three habits of mind repeatedly, because the habits enable leaders to initiate productive discussion-leading patterns appropriately. As a result, the leaders help the discussants find meaning in the text and defend the meaning with evidence.

Before proceeding further with analysis of the discussion transcript, let me mention one question that may have begun to trouble the reader—indeed, it troubled me as I was leading the discussion and even as I have reflected on the preceding excerpts. The issue is this: the introductory exchange with Michael was lengthy. In fact, it lasted six minutes and fifty-three seconds. During that time, other participants observed the conversation. Should others not have been invited into the dialogue before nearly seven minutes had elapsed?

I am still not sure about the answer to the question. Was that a mistake? We return to the issue in chapter 7, where we reflect on the achievements of the discussion.

For now, let us continue with our observations. The leader asks Eloise for her ideas:

SHG: Okay, now the issue here is why he forgets. Eloise, what would you say about this: In line 7 [it says], "He's forgotten the rules of long division." That's what it tells us, right? Has he [the schoolmaster] forgotten the rules of long division because he's getting older or because he's distracted by his wife's [having left him]? See, the evidence that Michael has pointed us to seems to be evidence for both of those things, right?

Here we see another discussion-leading pattern that experienced leaders frequently initiate: asking one participant, in this case, Eloise, to take a position on an issue that has been raised by others. In addition to re-posing Michael's question, the leader mentions that Michael has offered evidence for two resolutions of it. Eloise responds:

ELOISE: Yeah.

SHG: Or are you not convinced by that?

ELOISE: I see it, yeah. Like Michael, I see a parallel, but [it] is, like, a lot of the long division, like, has gone away from him, like his wife has. So and, like, you know, no one really knows why it's happening.

SHG: Why the long division has gone away from him?

ELOISE: Yeah.

SHG: And they don't know why the wife has gone away from him.

ELOISE: Right.

SHG: So what are they thinking about in line 32, Eloise? When it says they "look in silence at the schoolmaster?" are they looking … why are they looking in silence at him?

Eloise begins by agreeing with Michael that there is a parallel: "a lot of long division, like, has gone away from [the schoolmaster], like his wife has," meaning, it seems, that the rules of long division are like the schoolmaster's wife in that both have departed from the schoolmaster. Like Michael, Eloise looks for meaning in the poem by trying to follow semantic rules—trying to figure out who the actors are, the relations between the actors, and perhaps the rules that govern the creation of poetry as a genre. So Eloise mentions seeing a parallel. Again, Eloise, like Michael, does not explain how the presence of the parallel helps to resolve a question—the question of why the schoolmaster errs or some other question. Instead she says, "No one really knows why it's happening." Why what is happening? Is Eloise wondering, perhaps with the observers in line 32, why the schoolmaster has forgotten the rules of long division or why his wife has departed?

If Eloise is perplexed by the same things that perplex the observers in that line, then perhaps answering the original basic question will help her address her concern. Hence, the leader re-poses that question. If Eloise is not interested in addressing it—as Michael was not—she will not do so. Eloise responds as follows:

ELOISE: Well, I think they're kind of like … like, in awe of him, not really in awe, like, in observance because they don't understand really, like, how it is to get old and, like, they're observing how he's getting older like, how he's kind of like fading away, declining like Michael said.

SHG: So you think that when they look in silence, it's because they're trying to understand what it is to get old.

ELOISE: Yes.

Eloise suggests that the observers in the schoolmaster's classroom are watching him in order to understand what happens when a person becomes old. There is no suggestion, in her interpretation of line 32, that the observers are watching the schoolmaster in silence in order to understand the effects of losing his wife.

The question about the meaning of the text that Eloise addresses is different from Michael's. He eventually asked why the schoolmaster makes a mistake at the blackboard with long division, whereas Eloise addresses the question of what the observers in line 32 ponder as they watch the schoolmaster in silence. In answer to her own question, Eloise asserts that the observers are students and that they are "in observance because they don't understand … how it is to get old."

Another student has raised her hand, indicating that she wishes to enter the conversation:

SHG: Okay. Yes, please.

APRIL: When we read the line "We look in silence at the schoolmaster," I kind of see this as a reversal because for me to look at the name "schoolmaster," and you think about superior … [a] master is supposed to be better than his students and supposed to be leading towards growing up, which I guess also [is] getting older, and then by lines 5–9, "He's forgotten the rules of long division. Imagine not remembering long division!" So that's the student sort of explaining that [the schoolmaster] doesn't know what they know, but he was supposed to have taught them. He's moved beyond it and now they have the mastery of this sort of thing and I think it's sort of interesting the contrast between them growing older as in gaining knowledge and him growing older and losing knowledge.

April begins by quoting line 32, indicating that she wants to say something about it. She then makes her claim: the word "schoolmaster" suggests someone "better than his students." But, April says, she sees is a "reversal"—"the student sort of explaining that [the schoolmaster] doesn't know what they know, but he was supposed to have taught them." To April, the word "reversal" seems to mean that the students have changed places with the teacher and now know what the teacher once knew but no longer knows.

To support her claim, April identifies lines 5–9 but then reads lines 7 and 8: "He's forgotten the rules of long division. Imagine not remembering long division!'" She then interprets the lines: they are spoken by a student who believes "he" has surpassed the master—"Imagine not remembering long division!" the student narrator says. So, April has addressed the question of what the students are pondering at line 32 and made perhaps the best attempt yet to defend her claim with an argument that consists of identifying, quoting, and interpreting textual evidence. The discussion continues:

> SHG: Okay. So you would agree with what Eloise was saying … that this is really about his declining, but you're adding the idea that they … it is also about them gaining knowledge. It isn't just [about] him losing it, it's them gaining it.

Notice again that the leader says back to April what she has heard the girl say. Furthermore, we see evidence of another discussion-leading pattern commonly observed in experienced leaders. Listening to the contributions of Eloise and April, the leader relates the discussants' comments to one another, identifying a difference that she hears between them. Again, the leader seems to hear the ideas of both speakers in relation to the question that concerns both Eloise and April: what do the students ponder as they look in silence at the schoolmaster in line 32? Since both girls address that question, a shared point of doubt is beginning to emerge. By identifying similarities and differences that the leader hears in their views, she helps the members of the group refine their views.

Other discussants are awaiting opportunities to speak. The leader lists their names in the order in which she has seen the hands go up. Lisa is first in the queue.[9]

> LISA: Okay, well, I agree with April. Like, I think that what this poem is about is, like, the passing of the generations. Like at the beginning … in line 2 you have the schoolmaster looking out at the white trees, and then towards the end, you have the students looking out at him among the trees.
>
> SHG: Is that 32? Where the students are looking at him?

LISA: Yes, in line 32.

SHG: That's the students. The "we" is the students?

LISA: Yes. And, like, at the beginning, I see like the master is sort of … he's the master. He has mastery of the schoolhouse and the trees and knowledge, and then it all starts disintegrating … when he starts breaking the chalk and beginning the long division and throughout the poem [there is] this theme of him losing things that he previously had. His wife went away, he couldn't find the ticket, and then at the end, he's sort of fading away into the background into the white trees and his students are just there watching him.

Like Michael, Lisa begins by making a general claim about the poem. While Michael initially maintained that it was about the schoolmaster's "declining," Lisa declares that it is about "the passing of generations." Like Michael, she begins to defend her claim by turning to the "beginning" of the poem. She states that here, the schoolmaster is "the master," perhaps meaning that he is in control of things—"the schoolhouse," the "trees," the "knowledge." But then "it all starts disintegrating." Lisa sees a "theme" of the schoolmaster "losing things" that he once had. Again, we see a discussant try to find meaning in the poem by following rules—this time, by finding an idea that is repeated in the text, what she calls a "theme."[10] She lists the losses—the wife, the ticket, and the long division—a theme introduced by the schoolmaster's breaking of the chalk (line 5), she says.

Because Lisa has failed to identify, read, and interpret particular lines and explain how those lines support her claim that the poem is about "the passing of generations," her claim and argument are not clear. Her list of things that the schoolmaster has lost begins to support the idea that he now lacks things that he once had. But where is the evidence that a new generation has taken the place of the old, if the phrase "passing of generations" means that the young people now have things—skills, resources, knowledge, insight, perhaps—that the schoolmaster once had but now lacks? Or is that what Lisa means by the "passing of generations?"

To help Lisa clarify both the question of concern to her and the claim she wishes to make in response to it and to help her form a convincing argument based on textual evidence, the leader proceeds as she did with Michael. She focuses on particular line numbers, this time specifying one line:

SHG: So Lisa, what do you make of line 10, "We watch him with a different attention"?

LISA: I see it as sort of a sign of the students' maturing. Like, before, the schoolmaster was just the schoolmaster. He was the one that they listened to ... And now he's, like Michael said, declining.

SHG: So that different attention is what? What is different about it?

LISA: Different attention is ... they're seeing this different perception of their schoolmaster.

SHG: So they're seeing him as not just the person who knows arithmetic or whatever ...

LISA: But as ...

SHG: But as somebody getting older?

LISA: Yeah. He's undergoing the passage of time and so are they, and while he's declining, they're growing up. They're gaining the mastery of the things that he's losing. They can remember the rules of long division. They said, "Imagine not remembering long division!" and he can't remember it.

Lisa may grasp that the leader wants her to interpret line 10. Notice, however, that Lisa begins not by interpreting the words—she refrains from saying, in her own words, no more and no less than what the quoted words say—but inferring their meaning, namely, that the students are "growing up." Thus, the leader presses Lisa to interpret the quoted words more closely: "So that different attention is what? What is different about it?" Lisa repeats that the "perception"—the view—of the schoolmaster is "different."

What is different about the way that the students view the schoolmaster? How did they once see him, and how do they now see him? To interpret the line fully requires an answer to both questions. The leader offers an idea about the answer to the first question: "So they're seeing him as not just the person who knows arithmetic or whatever." Lisa's hesitation at the suggestion prompts the leader to offer an idea about the answer to the second question: "But as somebody getting older?" The suggestions that the leader makes are not arbitrary, as Lisa has mentioned both in her earlier comment.

At the end of the exchange, Lisa says "Yeah," indicating that the leader has understood her idea about how the students' view of the schoolmaster has changed.

Further, Lisa now seems to grasp what she needs to do to defend her claim that the poem is about "the passage of generations," for she explains both sides of it when she says, "While he's declining, they're growing up. They're gaining the mastery of the things that he's losing." To defend her claim, she almost takes the three steps needed to make a convincing argument based on textual evidence.

First, she provides textual evidence for her claim: "They can remember the rules of long division." In so saying, she gives an example of something that the students can now do and that the schoolmaster can no longer do, according to the text.

Second, she quotes the line that she has just interpreted in providing the textual evidence. "'Imagine not remembering long division!'" Lisa reads (line 8).

Third, she explains why the quoted line is evidence for her claim that the poem is about the passing of generations, a term she now defines: "They're gaining the mastery of the things that he's losing." Lisa continues: "They said, 'Imagine not remembering long division!' and he can't remember it." Here, she explains that the line supports her claim that the students can remember the rules of long division and they see that the schoolmaster cannot.

Lisa's argument begins to sound convincing, although she does not mention line numbers.

CONCLUSION

In the excerpts in this chapter, we have seen the leader follow patterns as she engaged the discussants in conversation. These patterns include the following:

- Pose the basic question to begin the discussion.
- Ask the participants about the meaning of the text.
- Suggest possible interpretations of the text.
- Ask the participants for textual evidence.
- Repeat back what the participants have said to confirm or clarify meaning.
- Ask the discussants directly about the meaning of their words.
- Ask the discussants to address comments or questions raised by others.
- Identify similarities and differences in comments and questions offered by the discussants.

How did the participants respond to the patterns initiated by the leader? What, if anything, do we see them learning to do? As has been argued, a successful interpretive discussion is one in which the discussants come to a shared point of doubt about the meaning of the text and make progress toward its resolution, using textual evidence. They must acquire certain skills and habits of mind to meet the goals of the discussion. Those skills and habits of mind include the following:

- Forming questions about the meaning of the text—questions that you cannot yet resolve.
- Making claims about the evidence in the text to answer the questions.
- Making convincing arguments that support these claims. Such arguments involve identifying places in the text that provide relevant evidence, interpreting the cited passages fully (saying in your own words no more and no less than what the cited passage conveys), and explaining why the evidence supports the claim.
- Listening so as to direct attention where it is needed, to exercise the above skills appropriately.
- Questioning what is said so as to listen appropriately.

In the next sections, let us see how the discussants in the preceding excerpts acquired these skills and habits of mind.

Michael: Beginning to Develop Interpretive Discussion Skills

Michael does not address the question with which the leader opened the discussion. Instead, he maintains that he sees a "reversal" in the poem and that the poem is about the schoolmaster's "declining." When asked to support his claim with evidence from the text, he mentions lines 5–9, which do support that claim. When asked to do so, he reads the lines. Without being asked to do so, he starts to interpret the lines, suggesting that he understands that he needs to explain in his own words both what the lines say and why they support his claim that the schoolmaster is declining.

Yet, Michael does not closely interpret the lines that he cites and reads. In fact, when asked for closer interpretation, he cites additional lines, which he does not read or interpret (lines 13–16). While these lines support a different claim—that the schoolmaster errs because he is distracted by the loss of his wife—Michael seems to recognize that a claim about the meaning of the text must be supported by textual evidence, and so he offers some. When asked to do so, he also cites and begins to interpret additional evidence (lines 25–28) that supports the claim that the schoolmaster errs because he is growing old. In short, Michael begins to follow and even initiate effective discussion leading and listening patterns, but his success is only partial.

Eloise, April, and Lisa: Watching the Growth of Interpretive Discussion Skills

Eloise has observed the dialogue between Michael and the leader, yet she does not pursue resolution of the question that Michael has opened—the question of why the schoolmaster errs at the blackboard—even when the leader asks her the question. Instead, Eloise begins by observing that no one knows why the schoolmaster made the error or why his wife has gone. In so saying, she returns to a version of the question posed initially by the leader: why the students are watching the schoolmaster in silence at line 32. Eloise argues that they do so because they are trying to understand the effects of aging.

Hence, Eloise fixes on a question about the meaning of the text and an idea about its resolution. Although the question had been suggested by the leader some minutes earlier, Eloise need not have returned to it. She does so, it seems, out of interest in it. And in so doing, she focuses attention on a point of ambiguity not easily resolved, as there is evidence to support more than one resolution. Eloise, unlike Michael, is able to focus on a point of ambiguity without shifting her question. She advances a claim about its resolution, appeals to evidence in support of the claim—indeed, evidence to which she may have been alerted, thanks to Michael's references to the schoolmaster's "declining."

April, however, not only seeks to resolve an interpretive question, but also makes a claim about its resolution in light of textual evidence. In addition, she recognizes the need to interpret the evidence. She begins her comments by quoting the line that she wants to interpret and thereby announces that she, like Eloise, wants to answer the question of why the students are watching the schoolmaster in silence in line 32. Her claim is that while a "schoolmaster" is supposed to be superior to his students—to know more than they know—lines 7–8 (which she reads) indicate that the students understand "that [the schoolmaster] doesn't know what they know." Here, April begins to interpret the quoted words.

Lisa accepts the question that Eloise and April have addressed—the question of what the students are pondering in silence at line 32. She says that she agrees with April's claim about the answer, explaining that the poem is about the "passing of generations." Although her defense of the claim is vague at first, she eventually offers a more forceful argument than did April. Explaining the meaning of line 10, "We watch him with a different attention," Lisa says, "Different attention is … they're seeing this different perception of their schoolmaster … He's undergoing the passage of time and so are they, and while he's declining, they're growing up. They're gaining the mastery of the things that he's losing. They can remember the rules of long division. They said, 'Imagine not remembering long division!' and he can't remember it." Here, Lisa not only interprets line 10 when asked to do so but also quotes a second line—the one April had cited. Lisa interprets it more fully and thereby defends the claim that the students recognize they know something the schoolmaster taught them—something he no longer knows.

Now, we must also ask, Has the group come to a shared point of doubt—a question about the meaning of the text that most, if not all, the discussants wish to address? We have already seen that such a question has begun to emerge. Does the dialogue between the Michael and the leader support its formation? And did the speakers make progress toward its resolution? These questions will be addressed in detail in chapter 7, where we return to the discussion of *Schoolmaster* held at the Aurora School.

Let us now turn to the discussion of "Rats" by Konrad Lorenz.

A Discussion of Konrad Lorenz's "Rats"

As noted in chapter 2, the essay "Rats," an excerpt from *On Aggression* by Konrad Lorenz, is a nonfictional, scientific analysis based on empirical observation. To interpret the text, the reader follows rules and, as Halliday says, identifies the characters in the text and the setting in which the action takes place. The characters here are rats of two kinds ("strange" and "residential"), and the action takes place in the territory of the residential rats.

As argued previously, lines 3–7 indicate that the residential rats respond aggressively when the strange rat "enters their territory," that is, when it locates itself in a place occupied by resident rats. But as you read on, trying to follow the experiential and interpersonal rules, ambiguities arise, as the discussants discover.

THE DISCUSSION PROPER

As described earlier, the students in Ms. Prentice's seventh-grade science class had not engaged in interpretive discussion on previous occasions, at least not in her classroom. In order to give all the students a chance to speak and listen, Ms. Prentice and I decided to divide the group so that ten students discussed the text while the others observed them, and then the observers became the participants while the others observed.[1] As it turned out, the first group in particular struggled to resolve the ambiguities about who the characters were and what they did. The discussants in the second group came to share a point of doubt that preoccupied Lorenz himself. (See appendix C for the complete text of Lorenz's essay and the cluster of questions prepared for this discussion.)

Let's begin by looking at an exchange that occurred among the discussants in the first group, who were contemplating lines 11–18 from the text. The lines describe what happens when a strange rat enters the territory occupied by another rat clan:

> The information is transmitted like an electric shock through the resident rat, and at once the whole colony is alarmed by a process of mood transmission which is communicated in a brown rat by expression movements but in the house rat by a sharp, shrill, satanic cry which is taken up by all members of the tribe within earshot.
>
> With their eyes bulging from their sockets, their hair standing on end, the rats set out on the rat hunt. They are so angry that if two of them meet they bite each other.

SHG: Okay, so let's have somebody start with, "The information is transmitted," … [and] tell us what it means and see if we can figure out who in the world we're talking about at the beginning of that next paragraph. Okay, Olney, do you want to do it?

OLNEY: Yes. [Reads first sentence.]

SHG: Okay, that's a long sentence. Let's go back to the beginning now. And let's just go up to the first comma in the sentence there … "The information is transmitted …" What do these words mean?

OLNEY: Like, they knew what's happening, so they weren't shocked by what's happening.

SHG: They … all right. So when it says, "The information is transmitted," you're saying the rats know what is happening.

OLNEY: So they aren't shocked by it.

SHG: And okay, what is happening?

OLNEY: That these other rats are coming that he can see.

SHG: So, "The information is transmitted like an electric shock through the resident rat." So what's going on here?

Here, the leader has asked the discussants to read and interpret lines from the text, and Olney has volunteered to do so. After reading, Olney says, "Like, they knew what's happening, so they weren't shocked by what's happening." The leader repeats back part of what she has heard—"you're saying the rats know what is happening"—which appears to be Olney's interpretation of the words she has read.

We see the student struggling to follow rules to determine who the actors are, what they are doing, and how they are relating to one another. The leader tries to help by following patterns that we have seen before. She repeats what she has heard the discussant say in response to the question of what the words mean, asking the discussant directly about the meaning and then quoting words that, if interpreted closely, might help Olney to clarify her interpretation. But in Olney's last comment, who is the referent for "he" that she speaks of? Is it the resident or the intruder? Another discussant, Malaysia, jumps in to "help" Olney by interpreting the quoted words:

MALAYSIA: He's warning them, "Don't touch me."

SHG: "He's warning them, 'Don't touch me.'" Who's doing the warning? Is that the resident rat?

CINDY: The resident rat is warning the rest of the family.

SHG: And why is the resident rat warning the rest of the family?

CINDY: He might think that … "Oh, I can beat him" … There might be, like, some baby rats and a mama rat, and she's like … "Don't touch my kids." She might think that the other rat is trying to invade and steal her babies.

Malaysia and Cindy may have different ideas about who is doing the warning. When Malaysia says, "He's warning them, 'Don't touch me,'" she may mean that the intruder is warning the residents, whereas Cindy declares that the resident rat is warning other resident rats. Neither Malaysia nor Cindy offers evidence from the text to argue her claim. Indeed, Cindy fabricates a scenario to support hers, seemingly unconcerned to find a basis for it in the text.

The text before these seventh-grade students is difficult for them to grasp. As we will see, I work hard to help them interpret the quoted words fully—to say in their own words no more and no less than what the quoted words say. It is not always easy to interpret quoted words fully, as we saw when reviewing the discussion of *Schoolmaster*. And it was not an easy task for these seventh-grade science students, who were inexperienced with interpretive discussion and were confronted with a complex text.

When discussants struggle to interpret a particular line, it can help to read aloud the sentence or two that precedes or follows the mystifying passage to clarify the referents—the actors, speakers, or recipients of the action; the nature of their actions; and their relations to one another.[2] Here, the leader takes the group back to the following sentence, which directly precedes the one in question (lines 7–11):

> The strange rat may run around for minutes on end without having any idea of the terrible fate awaiting it, and the resident rats may continue for an equally long time with their ordinary affairs till finally the stranger comes close enough to one of them for it to get wind of the intruder.

Mohammed reads the sentence and begins to interpret it:

MOHAMMED: They're all running around, right, … because they're all, like, panicking, so the resident rat is the one that comes and catches the wind with the intruder and so then, [the resident rat] alerts the whole clan or group of the rats.

Unlike Malaysia and Cindy, Mohammed uses textual evidence to address the question of which rat does the warning—the resident rat or the intruder. Mohammed infers that the resident rat is the one who does the warning, because the sentence he reads says that the resident rat smells the intruder and, as a consequence, warns the others. While the leader might have pushed Mohammed to interpret the line that he read more fully, the interpretation of the perplexing sentence with which they began lies ahead, so she presses the group onward:

SHG: Ah, okay, and then … one of the resident rats catches the scent and then the information is transmitted like an electric shock through the resident rat. Okay, so now what happens? Let's read the rest of this sentence. Mohammed, let's go on with this.

MOHAMMED: "And at once the whole colony is alarmed by a process of mood transmission which is communicated in the brown rat by expression movements but in the house rat by a sharp, shrill, satanic cry which is taken up by all members of the tribe within earshot."

SHG: Okay, so what's happening here?

MOHAMMED: It's kind of like … not really a battle cry, but it's kind of like a shriek, I guess, and so the rat would shriek, telling the resident rats that that's the intruder, and then so the other rats come, and they all kind of like jump in.

SHG: Okay, so they shriek. Okay, there's that sharp, satanic shrill … that's the resident rat who smells the intruder and he makes the shrill cry. Is that what you're saying?

MOHAMMED: Yeah.

SHG: Okay. Chauncey … I'm going to start reading from the beginning of the [puzzling] sentence. "The information is transmitted like an electric shock through the resident rat," who Mohammed says is the rat that lives there and the one who smells the intruder. Okay? And then, "And at once the whole colony is alarmed by a process of mood transmission which is communicated in the brown rat." What does that mean? Who is the brown rat?

MOHAMMED: The intruder.

SHG: Wait, wait. Chauncey, who is the brown rat?

CHAUNCEY: The brown rat is the intruder that the resident rat is alarming everybody else about.

SHG: Okay, so the brown rat is the guy who smells different?

CHAUNCEY: Yes.

Notice that Chauncey has accepted Mohammed's interpretation and has added to it by following its logical implication: if the "resident rat" is the one who smells the intruder and informs the others in his family of its presence through "a sharp, shrill, satanic cry," then the "brown rat" must be the intruder who does not smell like the others. The actors, their actions, and the relations between them are becoming clearer.

Recall the three steps that must be taken to establish a claim about the meaning of the text or some portion thereof: cite textual evidence that seems to support the claim, interpret the evidence (say no more and no less than what the quoted words say), and explain why the evidence, as interpreted, supports the claim.

Up until now, the discussants have been absorbed with an activity that takes place at step two—trying to say no more and no less than the quoted words, that is, interpret the quoted words fully. As we have seen, they are doing this to follow the ideational and interpersonal rules of the text and thus to identify the actors, their actions, the location of the actions, and the relations between the actors. So far, the discussants have not been working to identify an interpretive question about the meaning of the text that they wish to resolve—what I call a shared point of doubt.

Nevertheless, the leader has followed discussion-leading patterns that aim to draw them into text interpretation so that such a question has a chance to form. So let us now look at some excerpts from the conversation between those in the second group. Note that Cindy and Mohammed appear again, as they refused to become observers when asked to do so. Those in new the group play the name game and then proceed:

SHG: The floor is open. Okay, so Minnie [her hand is raised, thus requesting permission to speak], we'll start with you—and who else wants to do it?—and we'll go in that order. Cindy, do you want speak? And were you trying to raise your hand, Willie? All right, we'll start with you two. Okay. Go ahead, Minnie.

MINNIE: How does fighting benefit their survival?

SHG: "How does fighting benefit their survival?"

CINDY: I like that.

SHG: Okay, that's a nice question, isn't it? How does fighting benefit their survival? Okay, now when you say "their survival," are you talking about the survival of the ... of all rats or the family that we were talking about?

MINNIE: Yeah.

SHG: The family. Okay, so the family was invaded, and your question is, how does fighting benefit their survival? Okay, everybody understands that question? You might want to write it down, okay? And Cindy, did you want to ask a question, or what did you want to say?

CINDY: Like, why do they really have to fight? ... I don't understand, like, why they really fight because ... like humans, when somebody comes over to our house and they knock on the door, we're polite. We answer the door and we'll say, "What do you need?" but rats, they're, like, attacking people, and I don't really understand why.

SHG: All right, and so that's the question. And the way Minnie put it was, how does this fighting benefit the rat family's survival? Now, by "survival," do you mean ... how does the fighting help the family to stay alive?

MINNIE: Yeah, stay alive.

SHG: So I think [you two have] sort of the same question. Why do they ... why do they fight, and how does that benefit their survival? Is it your feeling that there's some place in the text where the author is telling us how the fighting benefits their survival, Minnie?

Notice that both Minnie and Cindy immediately pose a question about the meaning of the text for the group to consider. Their questions seem to be similar. Perhaps the time spent interpreting the text to follow the ideational and interpersonal rules and, thus, to identify the actors, their actions, the location of the action, and their relations to one another have now permitted a question about the meaning of the text to form. The conversation continues as the group tries to resolve the question:

MINNIE: Yeah, it was in, I don't know, the third page … 179 [lines 57–82].

SHG: Okay, so why don't you read the place that's suggesting to you some sort of answer to the question. Tell us where it is on the page. Read us the words.

MINNIE: It's a line … kind of towards the bottom or in the middle.

SHG: Is it in the first partial paragraph? Or is it in the second? … because they can't see what you're doing … Okay, so partial paragraph means that it doesn't begin a new paragraph. There is a place on the page where a new paragraph begins.

MINNIE: Yeah, it's right above that.

SHG: It's above where the new paragraph begins, okay. And you want to start reading from the beginning of the sentence, please.

It is important to help everyone locate the passage to which the speaker is drawing attention. When the font is small and there are many words per page, a leader should guide the participants to the location and allow them the time to find it. Once all are focused on the words in question, they may follow the discussion, that is, ponder the question on the floor in light of the passage.

MINNIE: Yeah. "On the other hand it is not impossible that as-yet unknown external selection factors are still at work; we can, however, maintain with certain—"

SHG: "Certainty—"

MINNIE: "—certainty that those indispensable species-preserving functions of intraspecific aggression are not served by clan fights." [65–68]

SHG: Okay, now, Minnie, we've got some interpreting to do here. So let's start with the first words that you read. "On the other hand," just, so take a group of words that sort of makes some sense, often up to a semicolon or up to a comma. Does everybody see where she is? Okay, this is important now. So you start with, "On the other hand,"

and take it as far as you want and then say in your own words, no more and no less than what the quoted words say.

MINNIE: "On the other hand, it is not impossible that as-yet unknown external selection factors are still at work; we can, however, maintain—"

SHG: Now, what does that mean? "Unknown external selection factors are still at work"?

MINNIE: Other options?

SHG: "Other options." But this phrase, "external selection factors," is actually a technical term. See if we can figure out what this could mean.

MINNIE: Doesn't "external" mean "outside"?

SHG: "'External' means 'outside'"? Anybody have any other idea about external? Can we agree that that's what "external" means, that it's outside? Yes? Nobody is objecting. Okay, so let's take it for the moment. It doesn't mean it's right. It's just we don't have anybody objecting, so let's take it. All right, so, "as-yet unknown external … " Okay, so some kind of … something from the outside. Now …

Here, the puzzling phrase is a technical term—a term whose meaning is specific, yet the intended meaning is not clear to the reader. Thus, the task is to study the text so that the intended meaning begins to emerge. Minnie has an idea about the meaning of the first word in the phrase—"external." She suggests that it means "outside," and so the leader asks the group if it accepts that definition. Since there are no objections, the suggested definition is accepted for the moment, and the group moves on to consider the next words in the phrase.

MINNIE: "Selection factors"?

SHG: Yes, now what are you going to do with that?

MINNIE: Other issues?

SHG: Okay, "other issues" … You said "external" means "outside." But what is a selection factor?

MS. PRENTICE: What does it mean to select something?

STUDENTS: To pick it, to choose.

So far, in an effort to identify the meaning of "external selection factors," the students have focused on their own ideas about what the words in the phrase might mean. Minnie has said that "external" means "outside," and that "selection factors" means "other issues." In answer to Ms. Prentice's question, the students, in a chorus, have said that "select" means "to pick, to choose." While some of the suggestions are helpful, they are not offered as a consequence of examining the text—of trying to see what Lorenz may mean by the phrase, given what he says. And so, the leader directs their attention back to the text:

> **SHG:** So when it says, "As-yet unknown, external selection factors are at work." Okay, remember what we're trying to do. We're trying to explain these words, and the reason we're looking at these words is because Minnie had the idea that perhaps in [the passage that contains these words], there would be some evidence that would help us to understand why these rats ... what purpose it serves for these rats to fight one another.

However, the discussants are not used to studying the text when they are in doubt about what it is saying. The discussion continues:

> **DURANT:** Rats are kinda vicious, by nature.

> **SHG:** Well, but how did they get to have that nature? And the question, the way Minnie put it was, "What purpose does [fighting one another] serve?" And in fact, that is what Konrad Lorenz is asking: what purpose does it serve? He poses exactly the same question, but about rats as an animal species.

> **MINNIE:** If they're always fighting, it's not gonna do anything good for them.

> **SHG:** Yes, if they're always fighting, it seems like it's not going to do anything good for them. So how do we explain the fact that they're always fighting? Okay, go ahead, Jack, if you want to.

In the preceding dialogue, instead of focusing on words in the text to see what Lorenz might mean by the phrase "external selection factors," Durant, reminded of the question on the floor, directs attention back to it. In addressing the question, he draws on his outside knowledge and says, "Rats are kinda vicious, by nature." In so saying, he retains focus on rats in general, as did Lorenz. But attention drifts away from Lorenz's words:

> **JACK:** Like rats, their natural enemy is snakes. So rats fight off snakes and ... because they've been fighting off snakes for probably generation upon generation, they're

probably really violent to the degree of fighting each other off. Like [they] spread the word out to the colonies that you can't be messed with.

CINDY: But doesn't that just kill the other rats in the colony? If they keep fighting, then it's gonna lower the population of rats … and then it's gonna lower the population of snakes because the snakes don't have any food.

MS. PRENTICE: Okay. We've got five people waiting to talk right now, so let's stop. That's good because it means that Jack said something that we can understand, right, and that we're excited about that, okay? … So who followed Jack?

GERALDINE: Me.

SHG: Okay, so, Geraldine, what did Jack say?

GERALDINE: He said that because rats are the enemies of snakes, rats have been fighting off snakes, so they're enemies, like violent toward snakes. [They are] enemies of strangers.

In the preceding excerpt, Cindy and Jack want to explain how intraspecies fighting among rats can help the species to survive, as did Durant previously. When two or more people try to address a question, a shared point of doubt is beginning to form. Cindy seems dissatisfied with Jack's answer, but exactly what has she understood Jack to mean? To help the discussants listen to and talk with one another, the leader asks Geraldine to say, in her own words, what Jack has said. After Geraldine responds, the leader says:

SHG: Okay, so they [rats] fight snakes. He [Lorenz] doesn't talk about them fighting snakes, so we're bringing in that piece of information and I don't hear anybody disagreeing with it. But because their natural enemies are snakes and they fight off snakes, does that mean that they get good at fighting off the snakes?

JACK: They get good at fighting and so, like, another rat comes in, they use that [opportunity] to protect their family [and] their food supply …

CINDY: So they might think that they're being harmed. Like, they're so used to, like, snakes trying to harm them and stuff. So when they see other strangers come, it's their instinct to fight because they think that something is going to happen.

Evidently, Cindy is beginning to follow Jack's reasoning now. She seems to mean that given their experience with other creatures like snakes over generations, rats by nature—"it's their instinct"—fight all intruders. If that is her meaning, it seems to be consistent with what Jack intends when he says, "They [rats] get good at fighting and so, like, another rat comes in, they use that [opportunity] to protect their family [and] their food supply." He seems to mean that the rats, by nature, will attack intruders to save family members and food because over generations, they succeeded by so doing.

> **SHG:** So the question here is, Do we see any evidence in the text for what Jack is saying? And Geraldine, I think you did a wonderful job of trying to say back to Jack what he had said to you. Can you say it once more? What was Jack's point?
>
> **GERALDINE:** That because rats have been fighting off snakes for generations, that it's their instinct to fight off enemies or whoever they believe is a danger to them.
>
> **SHG:** Uh-huh, that's what he said. Okay, so that's how they survived, right? For generations, fighting off these [other creatures] until they become better and better and better at fighting? Okay. Now, evidence.

Geraldine has done an even better job of stating Jack's idea than she did previously. She does not repeat his point that "they [rats] get good at fighting," but she seems to have heard it because she says the rats have been fighting those who threaten them "for generations," so it has become natural for them to respond to a perceived threat—an intruder—by fighting. Now, is Jack's hypothesis, embraced also by Cindy and perhaps Geraldine, one for which there is evidence in the text? Perhaps Minnie has found it:

> **MINNIE:** On page 178 [lines 20–56], and the third paragraph down.
>
> **SHG:** That begins with the words—
>
> **MINNIE:** It begins with the word "Without," but it's at the end of that paragraph.
>
> **SHG:** All right, but, you see, we all know which paragraph you're talking about now.
>
> **MINNIE:** "Only rarely does one see an animal in such desperation and panic so conscious of the inevita—"
>
> **SHG:** "The inevitability—"
>
> **MINNIE:** "The inevitability of a terrible death, as a rat which is about to be slain by rats. It ceases to defend itself." [46–48]
>
> **SHG:** So who are we talking about now?

MINNIE: And it says, "One cannot help comparing this behavior with what happens when a rat faces a large predator that has driven it into a corner ... In the face of death, it meets the eating enemy with attack, the best method of defense, and springs at it with the shrill war cry of its species." [49–53]

SHG: Okay, so what's going on in here?

MINNIE: So to defend itself, it has to attack because it can't do anything else.

SHG: All right. But what about the stuff you began with? "Only rarely does one see an animal in such desperation and panic, so conscious of the inevitability ... " Who are we talking about here?

CINDY: The rat.

SHG: Which rat? "Only rarely does one see an animal in such desperation and panic, so conscious of the inevitability of a terrible death."

CINDY: Well, it's talking about the intruder because [the text is] saying that very seldom, like, [do] you see the intruder come in and the other rats go to the corner and something. They don't just let the intruder do something ... that's very seldom, so you see the other ... the residential rat[s] attack.

SHG: Okay, so all right. Kimberly, do you agree with what Cindy just said? She's interpreting the sentence that begins, "Only rarely does one see an animal in such desperation and panic, so conscious of the inevitability." Do you see where I'm reading?

KIMBERLY: Yeah.

SHG: Okay. "So conscious of the inevitability of a terrible death ... is a rat which is about to be slain by rats." Which rat are we talking about here?

KIMBERLY: I think it would be the intruder.

SHG: It would be the intruder.

JACK: The brown rat.

SHG: And what does that brown rat do?

KIMBERLY: He stops defending himself.

SHG: So we're talking about two circumstances. One in which the rat, the intruder, is—it's so terrified, evidently, that it ceases to defend itself, right? And in the other case, we have a rat—and what situation is the other rat in? William? What situation is the other rat in?

WILLIAM: "One cannot help comparing this behavior with what happens when a rat faces a large predator that has driven it into a corner whence there is no more escape than from the rats of a strange clan. In the face of death, it meets the eating enemy with attack, the best method of defense, and springs at it with the shrill war cry of its species."

SHG: Okay, so we're talking about two circumstances. In the first one, which Kimberly figured out for us, the rat is so terrified it ceases to defend itself. This is the second circumstance. What is the case? What's going on in the second circumstance here?

WILLIAM: I don't know.

SHG: You just read it.

MS. PRENTICE: You can break it down, William. You can do it one line at a time, if it's too much all at once.

SHG: Start from the beginning of it. Okay. "One cannot help comparing this behavior with what happens when a rat faces a large predator." What does that mean?

WILLIAM: A big animal.

SHG: Okay, nobody's objecting? All right. "[A rat] faces a large [predator] that has driven it into a corner whence there is no more escape than from the rats of a strange clan." So what's going on with this rat? It's faced with a large animal, and what has that large animal done to him?

WILLIAM: Nothing.

SHG: It has done nothing to him? Huh?

WILLIAM: They trapped it.

SHG: Trapped it. What made you say they trapped it? What words make you say that?

WILLIAM: It's in a corner.

MOHAMMED: When the rat faces a large predator, it's like when the rat is gonna be eaten by a snake.

SHG: So the snake—it could be an example of the large predator, right? And it puts the rat into the corner. But what does the rat do under the circumstance where the snake or some other large animal puts it into the corner? What does it do?

MOHAMMED: It springs at it with a shrill war cry.

Although Durant and Jack had directed attention away from the text by asserting, "Rats are kinda vicious by nature," and "Like rats, their natural enemy is snakes," Mohammed returns to their claims to illustrate the meaning of the text. In so doing, he helps to clarify the comparison of a rat's response to two situations that Lorenz puts before the reader. The leader then summarizes the progress that the group has made interpreting the passage to which Minnie directed them.

SHG: Okay, so it [the rat] springs at it [the large predator] with a shrill war cry, "Yeow!" and [the rat] goes after [the predator], it attacks it, which is just the opposite of the sentence that Kimberly was reading, right? Where the rat ceases to defend itself. Okay, so we have two different responses on the part of a rat—two bad situations.

So according to the text, why does fighting benefit the family's survival? If you look at these two cases, one in which the rat just doesn't even try to defend itself, it doesn't fight, and one in which it takes on a big, a large predator—maybe it's a snake, maybe it's whatever, some kind of animal that backs it into a corner—and what does it do? It springs on the thing with a shrill war cry of its species. Can we get anything from looking at those two sentences? Do we get any idea about the answer to our question? The question, as Minnie put it, which is the question of how does fighting benefit the family survival? All right, Kimberly, we're going to start with you, and then we'll hear from Minnie and Cindy and William if he wants to.

Sadly, we must leave the story in Ms. Prentice's science class here. The bell rang and the tape was turned off, so we cannot know what the students saw in the passage they had been discussing. Might someone have argued that according to the text, the fighting response to an intruder, even if it were another rat, is more likely to help rats survive than the response of fear and passivity?

CONCLUSION

As was the case in the discussion of *Schoolmaster*, the leader followed patterns in order to help the discussants interpret the meaning of the text, form questions they cared to resolve, and make progress toward the resolution of the questions.

Once again, the leader repeated back things she heard the students say so as to confirm her understanding of their intended meaning. She asked them for textual evidence to support their claims, to read passages from the text that they identified, and to interpret the lines they read. She also directly asked about the meaning of lines in the text and the comments made by discussants. During the discussion, the leader asked participants to comment on the interpretations, comments, or questions offered by the others. She identified similarities and differences between questions and ideas that she heard. Finally, in the last excerpt, the leader summarized what had been said about the meaning of a passage and restated the shared point of doubt that the group had been working to resolve—two more patterns frequently followed by experienced discussion leaders.

Again we must ask, How did the discussants respond to the patterns? Did the students employ the following skills for a successful interpretive discussion?

- Form interpretive questions about the meaning of the text—questions that can be resolved in more than one way, in light of textual evidence.
- Make claims about the evidence in the text to answer the interpretive questions.
- Make convincing arguments that support these claims—arguments that involve identifying places in the text that provide relevant evidence, interpreting the cited passages fully (saying in one's own words no more and no less than what the cited passage conveys), and explaining why the evidence supports the claims.
- Listen so as to direct attention where it is needed, to exercise the above skills appropriately.
- Question what is said so as to listen appropriately.

As argued above, the students in the first group whom we observed discussing Lorenz's complex, nonfiction text did not arrive at a shared point of doubt about its meaning. Indeed, some had difficulty following the ideational and interpersonal rules of the text and so were unable to identify the actors, their actions, and the relations between them at moments. The opening remarks of Malaysia and Olney are cases in point. They were not asking interpretive questions.

At the same time, Mohammed and Chauncey seemed to follow these rules more easily, even toward the beginning of the discussion, and thereby helped the group identify who is doing what. Near the end of the discussion, Mohammed related one part of the text to a point made earlier in the discussion: "A large predator could be a snake." In so saying, Mohammed attempted to interpret the quoted words. He also showed that he had been listening to the conversation so as to interpret the text, perhaps with respect to the shared point of doubt.

Thus, the students in the second group began to respond with appropriate listening patterns so that a shared point of doubt began to form about the meaning of the text. Let us look more closely at some of the students. What discussion patterns did they follow? What skills were they beginning to acquire? Let us review how Cindy's discussion patterns evolved.

Cindy: Cultivating Some Skills of Interpretive Discussion

As mentioned, Cindy insisted on participating in both groups that discussed the Lorenz text. In the first group, she realized that the statement "The information was transmitted" meant that a resident rat was warning others. However, she failed to defend her claim with textual evidence and, instead, fabricated a scenario. It seems that at first, she was unclear about how to make a convincing argument using the text.

However, as the second group began its conversation, Cindy apparently arrived at an interpretive question she wished to address. She said that she liked Minnie's question, and her own was similar: Why do the families of rats "have to fight"? The question of why rat families fight one another perplexed several others in the group.

Cindy continued to cultivate her point of doubt. When Jack argued that rats fight off snakes over generations and become violent toward one another as a consequence, Cindy challenged his reasoning and argued that if the rats keep fighting the snakes, there would be fewer rats, and eventually, the snakes would have nothing to eat. So why does it benefit the rats to fight? Here, neither Jack nor Cindy were making claims about the meaning of the text. But both were trying to reason about the same question.

Eventually, Cindy began to follow Jack's reasoning when she said, "Like, they're so used to, like, snakes trying to harm them … So when they see other strangers come, it's their instinct to fight because they think that something is going to happen." Cindy was listening more closely to Jack and beginning to accept his line of argument.

Nevertheless, she fabricated an interpretation of the text instead of closely interpreting a cited passage. In the quotation "Only rarely does one see an animal in such desperation and panic, so conscious of the inevitability of a terrible death," Cindy saw that the line was in reference to the intruder. Yet, as argued above, she did not seem to grasp that two circumstances were being compared, and instead, she conflated them.

Overall, Cindy appeared to be learning to listen—to others and to the text. She followed ideational and interpersonal rules and was able to distinguish between the resident rats and the intruder. She came to an interpretive question she cared to resolve and followed the reasoning of another speaker who proffers a resolution. Yet, she was not yet committed to close textual interpretation to develop an argument for the claim that she defended.

Other Signs of Growth in Discussants' Interpretive Skills and Habits of Mind

Despite the difficulty that those in the second group had in addressing their shared point of doubt with claims supported by textual evidence that they quoted and fully interpreted, many of them exercised listening and discussion-leading patterns that moved them in the right direction. Had the group been given more time and experience with interpretive discussion, these patterns might have proved productive.[3]

For example, although Cindy conflated the examples of two rats' responses to perceived aggressors, Kimberly, Jack, William, and Mohammed distinguished the two cases, as they pursue closer text interpretation. In addition, they worked together, and with Cindy and Minnie, they formed and addressed the question of how fighting between rat clans benefits their survival. Furthermore, Minnie twice suggested passages from the text for the group to interpret—one that she believed offered evidence to address the question of why the rat families fight one another, and another to support the claim that a fighting instinct develops because it helps rats survive. Minnie, more than any other student, seemed to understand that sound arguments in an interpretive discussion are supported by textual evidence.

Geraldine made two attempts to restate what another discussant, Jack, said. Indeed, her second attempt interpreted Jack's statement with reference to the shared point of doubt of why rats fight one another, when she said, "Because rats have been fighting off snakes for generations, that it's their instinct to fight off … whoever they believe is a danger to them."

These students seemed to be learning to listen more closely—to themselves and to the text. And they were learning to form an interpretive question about the meaning of the text—a question they wanted to resolve. While limitations in their discussion skills and habits of mind are evident, their progress was evident as well.

Now, why did the first group fail to identify an interpretive question it wished to resolve? And why did the second group have no difficulty doing so? Furthermore, why did the students in the second group have trouble using evidence from the text to address their shared point of doubt?

In chapter 7, we reflect further on the discussion of "Rats" and address these questions. Meanwhile, we turn now to chapter 6, where we again see a group of inexperienced discussants try to understand a difficult, nonfiction text. Here, however, the group not only comes to a shared point of doubt but also makes progress addressing it through close text interpretation.

A Discussion of Toni Morrison's Nobel Laureate Lecture

We come now to the third of three interpretive discussions to be analyzed in this book. The discussants were a racially and ethnically diverse group of seniors at the Canterbury School—about eighteen years of age. I was told that they had never before engaged in an interpretive discussion. They were nearing graduation, and some but not all were planning to attend college. Some had struggled academically, and I was told that most came from lower to middle socioeconomic backgrounds. Prior to the discussion, I had met the group members informally on another occasion.

SETTING UP THE DISCUSSION

Both the discussants and I had prepared for our conversation by reading the text and writing questions about its meaning. I had developed the cluster of questions (see appendix D for the full text of the essay and the cluster of questions). We were a new group coming together to reflect on the meaning of a challenging text that was new to us all.

After learning their names, I asked the participants whether they would like to pose the questions they had written or whether they wished to hear my question.[1] Like the students at the Aurora School, they opted for the latter. I posed my basic question: Does the old woman come to trust the young people because she hears them trying to learn or because she hears them speaking the truth? The question is in reference to line 213 of the text, where the old woman says to her youthful visitors, "I trust you now."

THE DISCUSSION PROPER

The seniors at Canterbury School found Toni Morrison's Nobel Laureate speech of 1993 very perplexing indeed. Like the group discussing "Rats," they had difficulty focusing on an interpretive issue and spent the opening minutes discussing what was essentially an evaluative question. Let us look first at a few excerpts from that portion of the conversation to gain perspective on the progress that the group made over the course of the discussion, which lasted sixty-seven minutes.

As indicated in chapter 2, Toni Morrison begins her lecture with a story about an old, blind woman who is visited by a group of young people aiming to prove her a fraud—ignorant rather than knowledgeable. In response to their question about whether the bird that they supposedly hold is living or dead, the storyteller says the old woman's reply means "If it is dead, you have either found it that way or you have killed it. If it is alive, you can still kill it. Whether it is to stay alive, it is your decision. Whatever the case, it is your responsibility" (lines 32–34). Near the beginning of the conversation, the leader says:

SHG: What does [the old woman] mean when she says, "It is your responsibility?"

ALAN: I think she's saying, like, you should know right from wrong.

SHG: So that what?

ALAN: You should know what you should do and, like, ... if something was bad you should know not to do it, and if it's good then you should go on and do it.

SHG: So it's your responsibility to know right from wrong?

ALAN: Yeah.

SHG: Eban, do you agree with that? When [the old woman] says on line 34, "Whatever the case, it is your responsibility," does "it is your responsibility" mean that it's their responsibility to know right from wrong?

EBAN: Well, in this case, there's different people and every person has their own interpretation of what's right and what's wrong, so "whatever the case" may mean that whatever your case is from right from wrong, that's what you should go with. It's your responsibility. Like my term [interpretation?] of right and wrong may be different from Judy's interpretation of right and wrong. So it's my responsibility to take action for what I believe is right and wrong rather than Judy.

SHG: Okay. So you're supposed to take action for what you believe is right and wrong, and it means you're supposed to do what's right and wrong—or do what's right, I gather.

EBAN: Yes.

SHG : Okay. Is everybody agreed that that's what taking responsibility is? It's knowing what's right and doing what's right?

When the leader asks what the old woman means when she says, "It is your responsibility," the discussants respond. Alan says the old woman believes taking responsibility means knowing right from wrong. Eban, when invited to respond to the same question, says that taking responsibility means doing what you believe is right, even though someone else may disagree with your conception.

Here, we see that Alan and Eban do not answer the leader's question. Instead of studying the text to find evidence about what the old woman might mean, they draw on personal experience and explain what they think it means to "take responsibility." Although Alan refers to the old woman's view, he does not provide textual evidence to support his claim but, like Eban, seems to draw on personal experience to explain the meaning of the text. Both students evaluate the text rather than interpret it: they bring to bear their own criteria rather than searching for evidence in the text to discover what the old woman means by saying, "It is your responsibility." They are having an evaluative discussion.[2]

How does the leader respond? As in the discussions of *Schoolmaster* and "Rats," she follows several patterns—patterns aimed at helping the discussants interpret the text, even though they are not yet doing so. We have seen some of the patterns before. First, she asks them to clarify what they mean, as when she says to Alan,

"So that what?" Here, the leader encourages Alan to say more so that she can get a clearer understanding of his intended meaning.

Second, she repeats back what she hears: "So you're supposed to take action for what you believe is right and wrong, and it means you're supposed to do what's right and wrong—or do what's right, I gather." In doing so, she offers the discussants the opportunity to hear what she has understood them to say and to correct her interpretation.

Third, she repeats a question: "What does [the old woman] mean when she says, 'It is your responsibility'?" Repetition of the question helps keep it in focus and allows the discussants to target their remarks.

Fourth, she repeats ideas she hears and ask others if they agree with the ideas. For example, the leader repeats the question and asks Eban if he agrees with Alan's response that "it's their responsibility to know right from wrong." She then asks the other group members whether they agree with the ideas that she has heard Alan and Eban express, repeating their ideas in so doing: "Is everybody agreed that that's what taking responsibility is? It's knowing what's right and doing what's right?"

So even though the discussants are not yet interpreting the text but are stating what they think it means to "take responsibility," the leader follows patterns that aim to engage them in text interpretation. And what happens?

SONYA: I think it's change.

SHG: Hang on one second, Carl. Go ahead, [Sonya], and then we'll come right back to you, [Carl]. Go ahead.

SONYA: Well, knowing the responsibility that we have, we're here to change something.

SHG: And, so what is it to take responsibility? Or what does she [the old woman] think it is to take responsibility? To do what's right? What I heard Eban say was [that] each person may have a different idea of what's right, and your responsibility is to do what you think is right. Is that right? Eban, did I get it? Okay. So is that … are you agreeing with that, Sonya?

SONYA: Yeah.

SHG: You don't have to agree with it. It's fine if you don't. You said something about change and you may have something [else in mind]. It doesn't mean he's wrong. It just means that you have some other idea that we need to understand.

SONYA: I don't know … But she's [the old woman is] saying whatever the case, even … like sometimes whatever that case is, we still have the responsibility to change things. So, like, it doesn't matter what you think; it's what it's like believing what you think and what's for the benefit of everyone else. I don't know.

SHG: So taking responsibility is doing what is for the benefit of everyone else? That's another idea.

SONYA: I don't know.

Here, the leader hears Sonya use the word "change" and wonders if her position differs from Eban's, as he did not use that word. Because she is unsure, the leader asks Sonya directly about her meaning. In responding, Sonya, like Eban, repeats the old woman's words, "whatever the case." When Sonya tries to clarify her own intended meaning and explain why she used the word "change," the leader repeats back the idea so that the difference between Sonya's and Eban's positions can be contemplated by the group members.

The discussion continues:

CARL: Somebody said that responsibility is doing the right thing, always doing the right thing.

SHG: … Eban said, "What you think is the right thing," right?

CARL: But I can't agree with that because being responsible, to me, is, you do whatever you have to do to take care [of] whatever the situation is, whether it's negative or positive.

When he says, "Somebody said that responsibility is doing the right thing, always doing the right thing," Carl announces that he wants to address the issue of what it means to "take responsibility." In addition to stating the question of concern to him, Carl repeats back what he has heard someone say in answer to it. He is therefore initiating two patterns that, up to now, have been in the province of the leader. Larry amplifies Carl's position:

LARRY: And you're responsible for the negativity, too.

SHG: What does it mean to be responsible for the negativity, Larry?

LARRY: Like you have to face the consequences and then be responsible for them, for whatever you do.

SHG: Okay, I see you nodding. [Looks at Carl.] Do you think that's right?

CARL: Uh-huh [yes].

SHG: Okay, so you've got to face the consequences. [We have] more ideas now. We're not saying what's right here or wrong. We're just trying to figure it out now.

Thus far, the discussion has been evaluative rather than interpretive. That is, the discussants have not tried to explain what the old woman means by "Whatever the case, it is your responsibility." Yet, the conversation does become interpretive. In chapter 7, we return to the question of how the focus on text interpretation comes about and role that the evaluative conversation may have played in that transition.

In the following excerpts, the students address a question about the meaning of the text—a question that they become eager to resolve. They also make progress toward resolution by working together to interpret the text and, in so doing, gain facility with line-by-line analysis. The following exchange occurred soon after the one above:

SHG: So all right, so what is the truth that she [the old woman] recognizes that these children know, and therefore she's willing to trust them? She says at the end, "I trust you now." Sonya's idea was that she recognizes that they know some truth. Well, what is it?

TERESA: Well, I feel like she trusts them with ... the ability to question, which would lead them to truth because right now they don't ...have the truth in their hands, like how she says, you know, that bird is not in your hands, but, you know ...

SHG: What ... are you reading? From the very end again?

TERESA: Yeah.

SHG: So take us there again, what lines?

TERESA: This [is] line 214 [actually 213–214].

SHG: Two fourteen, okay.

TERESA [reading]: "'Finally,' she [the old woman] says, 'I trust you now. I trust you with the bird that is not in your hands because you have truly caught it.'" Like, they don't really have the whole truth in their hands, but they're beginning to seek it.

SHG: All right. And how does she know they're beginning to seek it?

TERESA: Because they're beginning to question her.

When Teresa reads lines 213–214, she begins to interpret the passage: "Like, they don't really have the whole truth in their hands, but they're beginning to seek it." By this, Teresa seems to mean that the bird stands for the truth and that the old woman is saying that while the young people do not know the truth ("don't really have the whole truth in their hands"), they are beginning to seek the truth.

Where is the evidence that the old woman comes to trust the young people "because they're beginning to question her" (Teresa's claim)? Larry points to specific lines, and he and Dave proceed with the line-by-line analysis, as the leader follows patterns to help them:

LARRY: "Our inheritance is an affront."

SHG: Okay, so 175, "Our inheritance is an affront."

LARRY: "You want us to have your old blank eyes and see only cruelty and mediocrity."

SHG: Okay, Dave, do you want to take this line by line? "Our inheritance … "

DAVE: "Our inheritance is an affront. You want us to have your old blank eyes and see only cruelty and mediocrity."

SHG: Okay, let's stop with those two. Why don't you start with the first one.

DAVE: Like … they're kind of saying, Do you want us to do like you did and turn out the way you are? It's kind of like …they want to take things into their own hands.

SHG: "They want to take things into their own hands." What is this sentence, "Our inheritance is an affront"?

In the preceding dialogue, Larry identifies and then reads lines that he believes provide textual evidence for Teresa's claim that the young people begin to question the old woman. But when the leader asks Dave to interpret the lines, beginning with the first one read by Larry, "Our inheritance is an affront" (175), Dave responds, "They're kind of saying, Do you want us to do like you did and turn out the way you are?" In so saying, he gives a vague interpretation of the second line that Larry read: "You want us to have your old blank eyes and see only cruelty and mediocrity." Dave makes little attempt to say no more and no less than what the quoted words say. He then adds, "It's kind of like … they want to take things into their own hands," by which he may mean that the young people are questioning, or challenging, the old woman. Here, Dave stops trying to interpret the quoted words and instead jumps to the conclusion that the lines provide evidence that the young people are questioning the old woman, much as Teresa claimed. But Dave has not yet demonstrated that such is the case. To do so, he needs to interpret the quoted words more closely. And so the leader asks, "What is this sentence, 'Our inheritance is an affront'?" That is, what does the sentence mean? The discussion continues:

> **SONYA**: What's "an affront"?[3]
>
> **SHG**: What's "an affront"? Any ideas? Go ahead, Dave.
>
> **DAVE**: I …
>
> **SHG**: Sometimes when I see a word [and] am not sure what it means, I try to read it in the context. So if you read a little bit more, let's come back, just as you were doing, Dave …"You want us to have your old, blank eyes and see only cruelty and mediocrity."
>
> **DAVE**: [It means] To think everything was, like, bad, like, see only the bad and the negative.
>
> **SHG**: Okay. "You want us to have your old, blank eyes." So that sounds like what?
>
> **DAVE**: To be blind like you and not be able to see …
>
> **SHG**: Be blind, be not be able to see … So they're saying, "You want us to be like you"? Is that what you're seeing in this? [Dave nods assent.] All right, so … what is this, "Our inheritance is an affront"?
>
> **LARRY**: And is it already negative?
>
> **SHG**: Already negative?
>
> **LARRY**: Well, like maybe passed down negative …
>
> **DAVE**: Like, what we're getting is no good.
>
> **SHG**: What's being passed down is not very great? Okay. So let's keep going. Let's see if that's going to work, because the test of whether it's the right [interpretation] is whether this whole passage as we go along continues to make sense. Okay, Dave, why don't you just keep going.

When the leader says, "What is this sentence, 'Our inheritance is an affront'?" she asks directly for interpretation of the quoted words. When Sonya asks, "What's 'an affront'?" the student initiates the pattern of asking directly about the meaning of a quoted word. The leader replies with a strategy for figuring out its meaning: reading and interpreting the words that follow the word in question. Focusing on it, Dave makes a closer, albeit partial, interpretation of the subsequent line, "You want us to have your old, blank eyes and see only cruelty and mediocrity." He says it means, "To think everything was, like, bad, like, see only the bad and the negative." The leader then asks about the meaning of the additional words in the sentence that Dave has begun to interpret. He responds, "To be blind like you and not be able to see." So, first asking about meaning, the leader then repeats back the interpretation that Dave has given.

The same familiar patterns—repeating back what discussants say, asking directly for interpretation of spoken or written words—seem to help Dave interpret the quoted words more closely. Here, as we saw in the discussion of "Rats," the discussants are asked to consider the context in which puzzling words appear to get ideas about the meaning and to test interpretations. By engaging in dialogue with the leader, Dave seems to help Larry as well as himself to interpret the text, and their responses to one another appear to help the leader grasp their understanding of the lines. By identifying, reading, and interpreting them as they do, Dave and Larry offer clearer textual evidence that the young people are beginning to question the old woman—much as Teresa has claimed.

But if the old woman comes to trust the young people because she sees them questioning her, exactly what sort of questioning brings about her trust? Is it the kind that Dave and Larry see here—a questioning of the old woman herself that amounts to a challenge to her competence ("to be blind like you and not be able to see?") and her accomplishments ("Like, what we're getting is no good")? In the next excerpt, Sonya comes to a new idea about the nature of the questioning that might have inspired trust in the old woman:

SHG: Does everybody agree [that the old woman comes to trust the young people because she sees them questioning?] … I mean, because she takes a real about turn [at lines 213–214].

SONYA: I agree with that.

SHG: Yes, why?

SONYA: Like, before she says, "'Finally,' she says, 'I trust you'"—like, there's this big chunk right here.

SHG: Yes, where are you?

SONYA: When they talk about slaves ... I couldn't understand that at all.

Sonya makes a move that is unusual for a discussant inexperienced with inter-pretive discussion: she draws attention to a long passage that has not been men-tioned thus far, and in so doing, she announces that she does not understand the passage. Thus, she takes the group to a place in the text whose meaning she says she does not grasp. Could it be that despite her uncertainty, she intuits something in the passage that she believes may help address the question of why the old woman comes to trust the young people?

Indeed, Sonya's move seems to be that of a seeker—someone who does not know, wants to find out, and is willing to chance the display of her own ignorance to make progress toward resolution. Perhaps, having heard Dave and Larry help each other address the question by identifying, reading, interpreting a passage, and then drawing an inference about the answer, she is beginning to trust that others will help her in a similar way. So what happens?

SHG: Okay, go ahead. Take it ... where are the lines?

SONYA: It's all this.

SHG: Come on, give us the line number.

SONYA: One ninety-seven.

SHG: One ninety-seven. Okay.

SONYA: "Tell us about ships turned away."

SHG: Okay, just one second, Sonya. Who is speaking here?

SONYA: I think ...

DAVE: The kids [the young people].

SONYA: It's the kids, yeah.

SHG: It's the kids. Everybody is convinced of that, the kids? Okay, so read us a little bit.

SONYA: "Tell us about ships turned away from shorelines at Easter, placenta in a field. Tell us about a wagonload of slaves, how they sang so softly their breath was indistinguishable from the falling snow. How they knew from the hunch of the near-est shoulder that the next stop would be their last. How, with hands prayered in their sex, they thought of heat, then sun. Lifting their faces as though it was there for the taking. Turning as though there for the taking. They stop at an inn. The driver and his mate go in with the lamp leaving them humming in the dark. The horse's void steams into the snow beneath its hooves and its hiss and melt are the envy of the freezing slaves. The inn door opens: a girl and a boy step away from its light. They climb into the wagon bed. The boy will have a gun in three years, but now he carries a lamp and a jug of warm cider. They pass it from mouth to mouth. The girl offers bread, pieces of meat and something more: a glance into the eyes of the one she serves. One helping for each man, two for each woman. And a look. They look back. The next stop will be their last. But not this one. This one is warmed. It's quiet again when the children finish speaking, until the woman breaks into the silence."

SHG: What is happening here now?

SONYA: They're talking about how, I guess, this group of slaves, they're in like some kind of a wagon and they know that, I guess, they're going to die. I still don't get how that connects to like … I don't know if she [Morrison] is talking about that specific generation of slaves and how they knew but they still made it, and maybe that's how she's connecting it to line 214 [213–214]. Like how they had it hard, but then their generation still survived and that they acknowledge that or they know that.

The preceding excerpt occurs fifty-three minutes into a sixty-seven-minute discussion. The conversation is nearing the end. Sonya has identified and read a large piece of text, and given the time constraints, it will not be possible to interpret every line. Thus, the leader allows Sonya to continue reading until a coherent portion of the text has been placed before the group. The leader's question must be, What evidence does Sonya see in the passage for answering the question of why the old woman comes to trust the young people? The question has become the shared point of doubt in the group.

The leader asks Sonya to interpret the passage she has read. Although Sonya mentions some facts presented in the story, she does not take the passage line by line and she fails to say no more than what the quoted words say. Instead, she presses on to state her point of doubt about the meaning of the quoted words, asking if the story is about a specific generation of slaves or all slaves. And she asks how the story told by the young people about the slaves brings about trust in the old woman. Sonya seems eager to answer these questions.

The leader responds:

SHG: So the young people are talking to the old woman, and they say, "Tell us about ships turned away from shorelines at Easter," and so on. "Tell us about the wagonload of slaves." Tell us. So, in this particular passage, they seem to think she knows something or has something to tell them. Is that right? And they're trying to find out about it?

Here, the leader's response comes as a consequence of pondering Sonya's words with reference to the group's point of doubt—the question of why the old woman comes to trust the young people. The leader repeats back to Sonya what the leader has heard the student say and asks for confirmation of Sonya's intended meaning.

SONYA: Yes. They're asking about this specific generation of people.

SHG: Uh-huh. And they're trying to find out about them?

SONYA: About how even though they went through that, how they came out … what was the aftermath of it?

SHG: What happened to the slaves? As though they don't know themselves and they think she does?

SONYA: Yeah.

SHG: What I'm hearing you say, Sonya, is that this [passage] is evidence or may be evidence—because we have to go through it—that the old woman comes to trust the young people because she hears them trying to learn something from her. Really asking because they don't know. Okay? It's another possibility that we could put alongside of the possibility that we've been exploring—that is, that she comes to trust them because she hears them speaking [some] truth, and [that truth], as was [stated] earlier, is that they recognize that the world's [not] so great, and as you put it, Dave, they want to do something about it and they care about it. Right?

In the preceding passage, the leader hears Sonya offer an idea about the answer to the shared point of doubt. Sonya's answer differs from the one proposed by Dave and Larry. By identifying similarities and differences between proposed answers to the shared concern, the leader keeps the question and the suggested resolutions in focus.

Which is the better resolution? For which resolution is there more evidence? Or is there yet another possibility better justified by the text than either of these two answers? Looking at the sentence that begins with "How lovely" (214) may help the group evaluate the strength of their suggestions, and so the leader turns the group's attention to the last words that the old woman speaks:

SHG: All right, but then she goes on to say, "How lovely it is, this thing we have done—together." What did they do together? Go on, Carl.

CARL: I don't know. "This thing we have done—together," like, I think they both grew. Like her in, like, seeing the kids, respecting the kids as trustworthy, smart, whatever, intelligent, and the kids seeing her as a wise older woman that knows what she's talking about. Anything else?

SHG: Yeah. He's asking exactly the right thing.

LARRY: I think that they all know that it's still—that their lives are still kind of messed up and they want to change it and they both realize that it's bad.

SHG: "They both" meaning [who]?

LARRY: The old lady and the kids.

SHG: But what's "lovely"?

LARRY: It's lovely that they know now and they'll try to change it.

SHG: They both know?

LARRY: Yeah, together.

SHG: They learned it together?

LARRY: Yeah.

When Carl says, "I don't know. 'This thing we have done—together,'" he repeats back the line that the leader has read. Perhaps he is announcing that he wishes to interpret the line—that he doesn't know what it means and wants to make sense of it in light of the question that has concerned the group. What, after all, was it that the young people in Morrison's story had done together, and why would the old woman trust them, now that they had done it?

As he continues, Carl tries to answer the question. He seems to say that both the young people and the old woman came to see something good in the other—something that they had not seen initially: "Like, I think they both grew." He describes what has changed about their perceptions of one another: "Like, her in, like, seeing the kids, respecting the kids as trustworthy, smart, whatever, intelligent, and the kids seeing her as a wise older woman that knows what she's talking about."

But what had the old woman and the young people done "together" that made them each acquire a new perception of the other? When Carl asks, "Anything else?" he may mean, Can anyone say more about how they now perceive one another and why? He, like Sonya, seems to be seeking help from others to answer the question of why the old woman has come to trust the young people and, indeed, as he now adds, why they have come to respect her. Here, we see clearly what happens when a group comes to share a point of doubt: the members keep trying to answer the question.

When Larry speaks, he seems to address Carl's question of "anything else?" Carl has argued that by talking together, the old woman and the young people have discovered mutual respect. But what is "lovely," says Larry, is the shared understanding of the world that they now have—"they all know that … their lives are still kind of messed up and they want to change it and they both realize that it's bad." Furthermore, says Larry, they came to the insight "together," meaning, perhaps, through the conversation. The leader wants to know if others believe that the text supports the suggestions that Carl and Larry have given:

> SHG: Anything else that you want to say about this? "Look. How lovely it is, this thing we have done—together."
>
> EBAN: I think what she [the old woman] means by that is, like, they both knew that they were both rather screwed up, you know what I mean? And then, like, but they still were able to learn something from each other, like … they both know the same thing, but they were able to learn it from different perspectives.
>
> SHG: So what did they each learn?
>
> EBAN: I'm not exactly sure. I can't read their minds.
>
> SHG: But you're saying this for some reason. You must have some sense that they learned that … when you say they both learned, then you have some sense of what each learned.
>
> EBAN: I don't exactly know how to explain that. [There is a] huge thought process that I go through …
>
> SHG: It's great. Let's hear a little bit of it.
>
> EBAN: It's a big process. It's kind of complicated, but it's like …
>
> ALAN: We've got time.

SHG: No, we don't have a whole lot of time. But you think that they both learned something and they learned it together, which was sort of Larry's idea—that this was something that happened together, right?

LARRY: Yeah.

The exchange above occurs sixty-three minutes into the conversation. Despite the time that has elapsed, Alan tells Eban, "We've got time" to hear about Eban's "huge thought process." So, while time is running out, Alan's concern to understand Eban seems sincere, which perhaps encourages the participants to lose their inhibition and express their uncertainty.

Like many people inexperienced with interpretive discussion, Eban seems to have an idea that he cannot easily express. Does he mean that both the young people and the old woman learned "the same thing" from their conversation, namely, that both they and the other were "screwed up"? And what does he mean by "screwed up"? To what evidence in the text does he refer? When he adds, "But they still were able to learn something from each other," what does "something" mean—that they were "screwed up" or that they could learn from one another?

To help Eban express his idea, the leader suggests that he relate it to one offered by Larry. Her suggestion meets with silence from Eban. But Alan continues to seek resolution:

ALAN: I think she's talking about not just about a bird but like, like, truth and knowledge, because you can't really hold truth and knowledge in your hand, but when you catch it, you catch it in your head. You learn from it.

Does Alan mean that the old woman comes to trust the young people because she sees that they have learned something—caught knowledge in their head, as he says? Is he returning to Teresa's idea that the old woman begins to trust the young people because she sees them questioning, trying to "catch [knowledge] in your head. You learn from it"?

SHG: You can't hold it in your hand.

SONYA: Yeah, so in a way, she went back to what they had said, and that's what she learned from them. When in the line 163, they say when …

SHG: Wait, wait, 163, 163 …

SONYA: One sixty-two … and then, like, when they're talking about the magic and when they say, "When the invisible was really magic … " No, no, I'm sorry. One sixty-one, above it. "Don't you remember being … " oh, I'm sorry.

SHG: It's a lot of stuff. I know, I know.

SONYA: Yeah, "When the invisible was what magic—"

SHG: Okay, read from the beginning of the sentence, please.

SONYA: All right. Where, 161?

SHG: Whatever sentence you like, from the beginning of it.

SONYA: Yeah, 161 then. "Don't you remember being young when language was magic without meaning, when what you could say, could not mean? When the invisible was what imagination strove to see?" So I think that she kind of understands that, and towards the end, that line [213–214] kind of supported it. Like, "I trust you with the bird that is not in your hands," but they have it. So you don't have to see it, but it … if they know it as in knowledge, then it doesn't have to be in your hand as long as you know it. So she kind of picked that up from them. So I guess she kind of turned it around.

The line Sonya reads from the text is spoken by the young people to the old woman. Perhaps it means, Don't you, old woman, remember when words uttered by you or others caused things to happen but you did not understand why those things happened? When you did not understand the things you saw with your eyes? When what you could not see with your eyes you tried to see with your imagination? Do you not remember these experiences from your childhood?

Without interpreting line 161 that she quotes, Sonya says, "So I think that she kind of understands that, and towards the end, that line kind of supported it." What does the old woman understand now such that she trusts the young people? The leader does not yet follow Sonya's reasoning and continues:

SHG: She kind of turned it around. So they're speaking … Are you trying to say what [the young people are] saying?

EBAN: No, it [line 213–214] is an old lady pushing back at them. Like, "You've come to me knowing I'm blind, saying that I don't know or trying to disprove me. And here we both are talking about trying to get to the same goal that none of us can see." Like, they're trying to find the truth and you can't physically see truth and it's kind of the, like, the unison of an idea: I can't see, you can't see, and we both still have nothing in our hands, but we both go for the same thing.

SHG: Even though … even though neither of us can see.

EBAN: Yeah, exactly. Yeah …

SHG: All right, so why does she trust them at the end? It sounds like what you're saying now is, "We're seekers and we've been seeking together, and because we've been seeking together, I can trust you." I think that's a pretty good morning's work. [Applause.]

In the preceding dialogue, Eban, who just moments before had declared that he could not explain his "big thought process," offers an answer to the shared point about why the old woman comes to trust the young people. Furthermore, his resolution is consistent with lines 161–163, which Sonya had quoted. In so doing, Eban initiates a pattern often initiated by the leader during the discussion: he tries to say, in his own words, another's intended meaning, in this case, the meaning of lines 213–214. He says, "And it's kind of the like the unison of an idea: I can't see, you can't see, and we both still have nothing in our hands, but we both go for the same thing," which seems to mean that both the old woman and the young people have come to recognize that none of them can see the truth about how to live and that at the same time, they are all trying to see it, or learn it. Because the old woman sees that the young people, like her, are trying to find the truth about how to live, she says that she trusts them.

CONCLUSION

In observing the discussions in here and in chapters 4 and 5, we watched students make progress with aspects of text interpretation during the conversations. In the discussion of *Schoolmaster*, three participants came to share a point of doubt and began to form arguments for claims based on textual evidence. In the discussion of "Rats," the second group came to share a point of doubt. Yet, this group had difficulty interpreting passages from the text to make progress toward resolution. In the discussion of Toni Morrison's Nobel Laureate speech, the participants come to share a point of doubt, seek help from the text and one another in addressing it, and work to evaluate possible resolutions based on textual evidence. Let's analyze how the discussion at the Canterbury School offers striking examples of individuals acquiring the skills and habits of mind needed for successful participation in interpretive discussion.

Eban: Learning to Listen So As to Interpret the Text and Address the Shared Point of Doubt

Early in the discussion, the leader asked, "What does [the old woman] mean when she says, 'It is your responsibility'?" The question calls for text interpretation. Yet, Eban responds with a statement that directs attention away from the text and toward what he means by "responsibility": "It's my responsibility to take action for what I believe is right and wrong." Perhaps Eban has not heard the leader's question, or perhaps he does not yet distinguish between evaluating and interpreting the text.[4]

Later in the discussion, Eban works hard to interpret what the old woman means by "Look. How lovely it is, this thing we have done together." His interpretation: "They [the young people and the old woman] still were able to learn something from each other." When the leader asks Eban what each learned, Eban demurs, insisting that he cannot explain his reasoning.

Yet, at the end of the discussion, Eban explains the puzzling lines 213–214 and garners applause from his peers when he interprets Morrison's speech to mean that the old woman and the young people have learned to seek the truth with one another, although none can see it clearly. For that reason, the old woman comes to trust the young people.

There is evidence, then, that over the course of the discussion, Eban is learning to listen more closely to the text and to the other participants. He is also learning to focus on an interpretive question that he cares to resolve and to address it by trying to interpret the meaning of the text. He points to passages he wishes to interpret and ultimately shows progress in saying no more and no less than what the quoted words say.

Carl: Learning to Solicit Others' Ideas

Carl, like Eban, seems to make progress listening to others and to the text. Toward the beginning of the discussion, Carl recalls another participant's statement with which he disagreed: "Somebody said that responsibility is doing the right thing ... But I can't agree with that because being responsible, to me [taking responsibility], is you do whatever you have to do to take care [of] whatever the situation is." Carl repeats another's statement and, in so doing, positions himself to state his own contrasting view.

Furthermore, Carl and Larry, through dialogue with the leader, clarify Carl's position. Indeed, Carl agrees with Larry's statement that taking responsibility involves "fac[ing] the consequences, and then be[ing] responsible for them, for whatever you do." While Carl is not interpreting the text at this point, his conversation with Larry and the leader offers a model of helping one another to form and address questions. That model, followed by many of the discussants as the conversation proceeds, eventually allows them to assist one another with text interpretation.

Indeed, it is Carl and Larry who focus sustained attention on lines 214–215: "Look. How lovely it is, this thing we have done—together." While Carl says at first that he does not know what the lines mean, he reads the passage aloud and then begins to explain its meaning in relation to the group's shared point of doubt: "I think [the young people and the old woman] both grew. Like her... in respecting the kids as trustworthy ... and the kids seeing her as a wise older woman that knows what she's talking about. Anything else?"

Although Carl has begun to interpret the quoted line by saying that the "lovely thing" is the respect that the old woman and the young people have developed for each other, he seems to realize that he has not interpreted its meaning fully, for he invites his peers to add to his interpretation when he says, "Anything else?" Perhaps more than any other participant, Carl leads the others in working together to interpret lines they do not grasp at first.

Sonya: Becoming a Seeker

From the beginning, Sonya is not afraid to say that she does not understand. She declares that she does not know what the old woman means by "Whatever the case, it's your responsibility." Faced later with a puzzling word, she inquires, "What's 'an affront'?" She seems to discover that in an interpretive discussion, parading one's ignorance is rewarded by an increase in understanding. Later, for example, she brings up the story the young people tell the old women about slaves: "I couldn't understand that at all." When asked by the leader to do so, Sonya supplies a line number, reads the puzzling passage, and then begins to interpret it. Pressed for time, she hurries to pose her point of doubt again before the discussion is over: how does the story explain why the old woman comes to trust the young people?

We see evidence that Sonya has become a seeker—that over time, she forms a question about the meaning of the text that she wishes to answer. She identifies passages that she believes may prove enlightening and works to connect her incipient understanding of them to resolve the question. Time is running out, and Sonya hurries to remind the group of the goal—interpreting the text so as to resolve the question.

By putting a felt question before the group as she does toward the end of the discussion, Sonya seems to inspire Carl and Larry, and eventually Alan and Eban, to keep working for a closer interpretation of the text to resolve the issue. As Sonya turns their attention to additional lines (beginning at 161), she points the group toward the key to answering genuine questions, namely, working together to explain passages in the text—to interpret them fully—to get ideas about answers and evidence to support the answers.

If, as we have seen, Eban, Carl, and Sonya make progress developing the skills and habits of mind needed for successful discussion participation in the space of one interpretive discussion, imagine the progress they could make if given such opportunities on a regular basis.[5]

Chapter 7 addresses the following questions about what happened at the Canterbury School: did the initial, evaluative conversations help move the group members toward the interpretive focus they eventually assumed? How did the group move from evaluating the text to interpreting it? Why was the group successful in using textual evidence to address its shared question? In addition to these questions, chapter 7 reflects overall on what happened in each of the three examples of interpretive discussions. It asks questions about the formation of a shared point of doubt and progress toward its resolution.

PART THREE

Reflection

Reflecting on Three Interpretive Discussions

7

P<small>ART</small> 3 <small>REPRESENTS</small> the third phase of interpretive discussion—reflection. In chapter 7, we look back upon the cases that we observed in chapters 4, 5, and 6. In reflecting on each case, we begin with the questions that arose in our analysis of it.

For all three texts that we discussed in the book—*Schoolmaster*, "Rats," and Toni Morrison's speech—we ask two questions: Did a shared point of doubt emerge in the discussion—a question that many, if not all in the group, worked to resolve? Did the group make progress toward resolution? The clusters of questions prepared beforehand, the discussion-leading patterns, and the flow of ideas that emerged provide further perspective on what happened in each case.

SCHOOLMASTER

In chapter 4, we asked, *Should the leader have invited other discussants besides Michael to enter the discussion before nearly seven minutes had elapsed?* The answer to the question depends on the answer to two others, namely, did a shared point of doubt emerge in the discussion, and did the participants make progress toward resolution? In short, did the dialogue between the leader and Michael abort or abet the goals of the discussion?

As argued in chapter 2, a reader may find many points of ambiguity in the poem *Schoolmaster* by trying to understand the characters, their actions, and so forth. In chapter 4, Michael wonders why the schoolmaster makes a mistake on the blackboard (line 9) as he teaches the students long division. The question that concerns Michael does not become the shared point of doubt in the discussion. So, you might argue that his seven-minute dialogue with the leader was unjustified, since his question, which took time to develop, was not pursued by others.

But did a shared point of doubt emerge in the conversation? And if so, did the opening dialogue between the Michael and the leader help it to form?

Recall the initial comment made by Eloise, the first speaker to enter the conversation after the dialogue between Michael and the leader:

> ELOISE: I see it, yeah. Like Michael, I see a parallel, but [it] is, like, a lot of the long division has gone away from him [the schoolmaster], like his wife has … [N]o one really knows why it is happening.

In her last remark, Eloise directs attention to the observers in the poem: they are wondering what is happening to the schoolmaster, as both his knowledge of long division and his wife have departed, and they do not know why. In so saying, Eloise moves away from Michael's question of why the schoolmaster makes a mistake with long division at the blackboard. Her shift prompts the leader to restate the basic question of the prepared cluster, which asks what those observing the schoolmaster are pondering. The leader says:

> SHG: So what are they [observers or students] thinking about in line 32, Eloise? When it says they "look in silence at the schoolmaster?" … why are they looking in silence at him?

The original form of the basic question was, "Do the students watch the schoolmaster in silence (32) because they are trying to understand the effects of growing old or the effects of losing one's wife?" By re-posing the question (albeit in open form, that is, in a form that suggests no ideas about the resolution), the leader tests her hunch about the question that concerns Eloise. If Eloise addresses the proposed quandary, her deepest point of doubt may concern the observers of the schoolmaster rather than the schoolmaster himself. The exchange that follows suggests that this is the case:

ELOISE: Well, I think they're kind of like ... in awe of him, not really in awe, like, in observance because they don't understand really, like, how it is to get old and, like, they're observing how he's getting older like, how he's kind of like fading away, declining like Michael said.

SHG: So you think that when they look in silence, it's because they're trying to understand what it is to get old.

ELOISE: Yes.

SHG: When you're seeing somebody get old and this is declining and they don't really know what that's about?

ELOISE: Yeah.

Here, Eloise makes no attempt to shift attention back to the question of why the schoolmaster errs. Instead, she keeps the focus on the observers and repeats one of the possibilities suggested in the leader's initial basic question—that the observers are students and that the students watch the schoolmaster in silence because they are trying to understand what happens to people when they grow old.

And yet, Eloise mentions Michael twice. In the first instance, she says that she, like Michael, sees a "parallel" in the poem. In the second reference to Michael, she repeats the word "declining," and in so doing, quotes Michael directly, acknowledging that she has heard him use the word. She argues that the students see that their teacher is aging, which involves "fading away," and that "fading away" means "declining like Michael said." Not only has Eloise heard Michael's word, but she also believes it helps her express what concerns the students and, therefore, what helps her answer the question of why they look in silence at the schoolmaster—the issue she chooses to address.

April, like Eloise, continues to question what the observers in line 32 are pondering.

APRIL: When we read the line "We look in silence at the schoolmaster, " I kind of see this as a reversal ... [a] master is supposed to be better than his students and supposed to be leading towards growing up, which I guess also [is] getting older, and then by lines [7–8], "He's forgotten the rules of long division. Imagine not remembering long division!" So that's the student sort of explaining that [the schoolmaster] doesn't know what they know, but he was supposed to have taught them. He's moved beyond it and now they have the mastery of this sort of thing and I think it's sort of interesting the contrast between them growing older as in gaining knowledge and him growing older and losing knowledge.

When April quotes line 32, she indicates that she wants to focus attention on the meaning of that line. Here, we see a shared point of doubt beginning to form: first Eloise and now April are trying to explain what the observers are pondering at line 32. The argument April begins to mount suggests that her idea differs from the one given by Eloise, who averred that the students are trying to understand what happens to people when they grow old. April's idea seems to be that the students are pondering their relation to the schoolmaster with respect to aging.

When April enters the conversation, she uses the word "reversal." She does not mention Michael's name. However, the reader will recall that the word was first used by Michael at the start of his dialogue with the leader. Unsure about what he meant by the term, the leader questioned him about it. When April uses the word, she makes clear that a "reversal" occurs when characters have changed places: at first, the schoolmaster knew long division and the students did not; now, they know it and he does not. Did the dialogue between Michael and the leader help April to develop her notion of "reversal," perhaps?

Lisa, the next speaker to enter the conversation, also seems to share the point of doubt with Eloise and April:

> LISA: Okay, well, I agree with April. Like I think that what this poem is about is, like, the passing of the generations. Like at the beginning ... in line 2 you have the schoolmaster looking out at the white trees, and then towards the end, you have the students looking out at him among the trees.
>
> SHG: Is that 32? Where the students are looking at him?
>
> LISA: Yes, in line 32.
>
> SHG: That's the students. The "we" is the students?

Lisa begins with the claim that the poem is about the passing of generations. She says that she hears April arguing the same claim. Lisa's answers to the leader's questions indicate that she sees a connection between the schoolmaster looking at the trees at the start of the poem and the observers watching him at line 32 and perhaps thereafter. In addition, like Eloise and April, Lisa understands the observers to be students in the teacher's classroom.

As detailed in chapter 4, however, Lisa's argument in support of her claim is not convincing at first. Hence, the leader encourages her to interpret a line of the text that, if understood, might supply useful evidence:

SHG: Lisa, what do you make of line 10, "We watch him with a different attention"?

LISA: I see it as sort of a sign of the students' maturing. Like, before, the schoolmaster was just the schoolmaster. He was the one that they listened to … . And now he's, like Michael said, declining.

SHG: So that different attention is what? What is different about it?

LISA: Different attention is … they're seeing this different perception of their schoolmaster.

SHG: So they're seeing him as not just the person who knows arithmetic or whatever …

LISA: But as …

SHG: But as somebody getting older?

LISA: Yeah. He's undergoing the passage of time and so are they, and while he's declining, they're growing up. They're gaining the mastery of the things that he's losing. They can remember the rules of long division. They said, "Imagine not remembering long division!" and he can't remember it.

The dialogue between Michael and the leader seems to have influenced Lisa's thinking. When her attention is directed to line 10, Lisa repeats the word "declining," acknowledging that she heard Michael use it. She then utilizes Michael's contribution to interpret line 10 and explain what the students mean by saying that their attention to the schoolmaster is now "different" than it once was—"different" because they now see him as growing old, or "declining." By interpreting line 10, Lisa provides more evidence for her claim that the poem is about "the passing of generations."

In summary, Eloise, April, and Lisa have apparently begun to form a shared point of doubt. While it differs from the one that concerned Michael, they all mentioned him or something he said, suggesting that they believed they understood him. The perception that they understood him may have occurred because the meaning of Michael's statements were questioned by the leader to the point where other discussants could follow the statements and consider their merit. Perhaps the initial dialogue helped Michael clarify his remarks and begin to support his claims with evidence.

Having prepared the cluster of questions, the leader not only could propose a point of ambiguity about the poem at the start of the discussion, but also could hear what the discussants said in relation to that question when they returned to it, as well as other questions that they raised.

For example, the leader asks Michael for the line numbers that indicate the schoolmaster is "declining," Michael's initial claim. In fact, his idea is explored by follow-up questions 4, 5, 6, and 7 of the cluster (see chapter 3). Hence, the leader, having written the questions, is aware that there is textual evidence to support his claim. When Michael offers line numbers that support another claim instead—that the schoolmaster is distracted by the departure of his wife—the leader reminds him that he has had both ideas. The idea that the schoolmaster is distracted and errs because "his wife has gone away" is explored in follow-up questions 1, 2, and 3 of the prepared cluster.

The fact that the leader had developed a cluster of questions and had previously reflected on ideas that turn out to be of interest to Michael may have helped her exercise the three habits of mind identified in chapter 4. First, she was able to question him about what he meant by asking for textual evidence that she knew was relevant to his claims. Second, she was able to hear his ideas about his question of concern as it emerged in the conversation, because the question was related to an idea she had explored in the cluster (the departure of the schoolmaster's wife). Third, the leader helped Michael link his ideas to supporting passages, interpret the passages, and thereby begin to make arguments in support of his claims.

Having prepared the cluster of questions, the leader could follow useful discussion-leading patterns and thereby exercise the productive habits of mind. And by so doing, she probably helped the discussants, including Michael himself, grasp what Michael was saying so that when they entered the dialogue, they could also use his ideas in developing their own.

"RATS"

In chapter 5, we first asked, *Why did the students in the first discussion group fail to identify a shared point of doubt?*

While those in the first group had questions about the text, many of the questions were not interpretive. They could be answered in one way only, given the evidence in the text, and hence were what the Great Books Foundation calls "fact" questions.[1] For example:

SHG: So, "The information is transmitted like an electric shock through the resident rat." So what's going on here?

MALAYSIA: He's warning them, "Don't touch me."

SHG: "He's warning them, 'Don't touch me.'" Who's doing the warning? Is that the resident rat?

CINDY: The resident rat is warning the rest of the family.

SHG: And why is the resident rat warning the rest of the family?

CINDY: He might think that … "Oh, I can beat him" … There might be, like, some baby rats and a mama rat, and she's like … "Don't touch my kids." She might think that the other rat is trying to invade and steal her babies.

When the leader asks, "Who's doing the warning?" she asks a factual question, as the textual evidence for its resolution is definitive. Thus, the question can be resolved without debate provided the respondent can follow what Halliday calls the ideational and interpersonal rules of the text.[2] Cindy knows the answer to the question and gives it. The second question posed by the leader, "And why is the resident rat warning the rest of the family?" is also a factual question: the text makes clear that the resident rat warns the others because the animal has picked up the scent of a stranger (appendix C, lines 10–15). Cindy, however, does not provide the answer indicated by the text but instead speculates on an answer.

Cindy's response to the second factual question underscores the difficulty that many of the students in the first discussion group had with the text: they found it hard to follow the semantic rules that govern its meaning. That is, the discussants were not always able to determine who was doing what or how the characters were related to one another. These problems persisted as the students in the first group conversed.

Why did those in the first group fail to arrive at a shared point of doubt about the meaning of the text? The evidence in the transcript suggests that they were preoccupied with trying to follow the rules to grasp the facts of the text. While the first group did not come to share an interpretive question it wished to resolve, the group did become clearer about who the actors were, what they did, and their relations to one another.

Thus, we come to the second and third questions raised in chapter 5: *Why did those in the second group have no difficulty coming to a shared question about the meaning of the text? At the same time, why, having formed the point of doubt, did the second group have trouble addressing it with evidence from the text?*

Minnie and Cindy, who open the conversation in the second group, raise two interpretive questions. In fact, the questions appear to be nearly the same: Why do rats respond to the presence of a strange rat by fighting, or how does that response help a family of rats to survive?

As discussed in chapter 5, the first group's painstaking efforts to follow the semantic rules of the text may have allowed that the second group to raise the interpretive question. The suggestion has plausibility. In the first group, Cindy sees that "The information is transmitted like an electric shock through the resident" means that the resident rat rather than the intruder is doing the warning. Once Cindy identifies the fact in the text, no further question about who does the warning is raised. In the subsequent exchange, Mohammed and Chauncey do not hesitate in asserting that the "brown rat" is the intruder—another fact in the text, given the textual evidence.

Because the discussants in the first group identify the fact that resident rats respond to an intruder by alarming one another and preparing to fight, is it not surprising that Minnie, a discussant in group two, begins the conversation by asking why rats in a family respond to the presence of a stranger with negative aggression. Indeed, Minnie's question seems to have been opened by the conversation between those in the first group.

So much seems plausible. But why, having posed that provocative interpretive question, do the discussants in the second group have difficulty pursing its resolution through further study of the text?

The pattern of drawing on imagined scenarios rather than close study of the text persists throughout the discussion. Above, Cindy does just that when the leader asks her why the resident rat warns the rest of the family. A similar thing happens when Minnie poses her initial question. The leader asks for evidence from the text that addresses the issue, and Minnie cites and reads from the excerpt (see appendix C, lines 65–67), after which the leader asks her to interpret the words that she has read:

> SHG: Okay, now, Minnie, we've got some interpreting to do here. So let's start with the first words that you read … [T]ake a group of words that sort of makes some sense, often up to a semicolon or up to a comma. Does everybody see where she is? Okay, this is important now. So you start with, "On the other hand," and take it as far as you want and then say in your own words, no more and no less than what the quoted words say.
>
> MINNIE: "On the other hand, it is not impossible that as-yet unknown external selection factors are still at work; we can, however, maintain—"
>
> SHG: Now, what does that mean? "Unknown external selection factors are still at work"?
>
> MINNIE: Other options?
>
> SHG: "Other options." But this phrase, "external selection factors," is actually a technical term. See if we can figure out what this could mean.
>
> MINNIE: Doesn't "external" mean "outside"?

Here, the leader tries to focus Minnie's attention on the phrase "external selection factors," having told her, "we've got some interpreting to do here." The leader explains how to interpret the text ("just … take a group of words that sort of makes some sense"). Yet, Minnie guesses at the meaning of "external selection factors": "Other options?" she asks. She does not attempt to quote and interpret lines that might give clues to the meaning of the puzzling phrase. Eventually, Durant changes the course of the conversation with an evaluative comment—a comment that draws the attention of the group away from the text:

> DURANT: Rats are kinda vicious, by nature … Like rats, their natural enemy is snakes. So rats fight off snakes and … because they've been fighting off snakes for probably generation upon generation, they're probably really violent to the degree of fighting each other off. Like [they] spread the word out to the colonies that you can't be messed with.

CINDY: But doesn't that just kill the other rats in the colony? If they keep fighting, then it's gonna lower the population of rats ... and then it's gonna lower the population of snakes because the snakes don't have any food.

Durant draws on ideas that he has formed from experience outside of studying the text. Jack, like Durant, appeals to his personal experience, which is why both comments direct attention away from text interpretation and hence are *evaluative* comments.[3]

As described earlier, both Cindy and Geraldine begin to follow Jack's evolutionary line of reasoning and so address the question of why the rats fight one another. When they, like Durant and Jack, do not appeal to the text for evidence, the leader presses them to do so. Eventually, Minnie reads aloud this excerpt from the text: "Only rarely does one see an animal in such desperation and panic so conscious of the inevitability of a terrible death, as a rat which is about to be slain by rats. It ceases to defend itself" (46–48):

SHG: So who are we talking about now?

MINNIE: And it says, "One cannot help comparing this behavior with what happens when a rat faces a large predator that has driven it into a corner ... In the face of death, it meets the eating enemy with attack, the best method of defense, and springs at it with the shrill war cry of its species." [49–53]

SHG: Okay, so what's going on in here?

MINNIE: So to defend itself, it has to attack because it can't do anything else.

SHG: All right. But what about the stuff you began with? "Only rarely does one see an animal in such desperation and panic, so conscious of the inevitability ... " Who are we talking about here?

CINDY: The rat.

SHG: Which rat? "Only rarely does one see an animal in such desperation and panic, so conscious of the inevitability of a terrible death."

CINDY: Well, it's talking about the intruder because [the text is] saying that very seldom, like, [do] you see the intruder come in and the other rats go to the corner and something. They don't just let the intruder do something ... that's very seldom, so you see the other ... the residential rat[s] attack.

While Cindy recognizes that the rat in question is the intruder, she does not try to interpret the meaning of the quoted words closely. The quoted words seem to mean that only infrequently does one witness anxiety equal to that of a rat about to be slaughtered by members of its own species. However, Cindy interprets the words differently: "Very seldom, like, [do] you see the intruder come in and the other rats go to the corner and something." Indeed, Cindy does not seem to recognize that the text is comparing two very different responses to the presence of danger. Instead, she runs them together. The leader recognizes that Cindy, Minnie, William, and others are unaccustomed to close textual analysis. Thus, she tries to assist the members of the second group with an unfamiliar task.

Even without access to the remainder of the discussion, we do have enough of the transcript to address why, having identified an interpretive question about the meaning of the text, the second group had difficulty trying to resolve it using textual evidence. After the discussants identified some textual evidence and read the lines, they were not accustomed to saying, in their own words, no more and no less than what the quoted words said.

Could the coleaders could have helped the group find and more fully interpret relevant passages in the text? The complete cluster prepared prior to the discussion appears in appendix C. The basic question—"According to the text, why do rat clans hate one another?"—is similar to the shared point of doubt that intrigued the second group and, indeed, Lorenz himself. Consider follow-up question 2:

> When Lorenz says, "This good old Darwinian train of thought can only be applied where the causes which induce selection derive from the extraspecific environment" [56–58], does it mean that if hatred between rat clans is explained by saying it makes the rats more likely to survive, then the threat to their survival must come from outside their species? If so, do rat clans hate one another because by hating and fighting a strange rat who invades their territory, they practice a survival mechanism acquired through facing and defeating threats to their species over generations?

The question identifies and interprets textual evidence that helps explain why rat clans fight one another. A similarly relevant question is posed by number 7. Both questions suggest that if there is an evolutionary answer to the survival question, then the cause must be sought outside the rat species itself.

Interestingly enough, the passage referred to in questions 2 and 7 invites speculation about the extraspecific force—the cause coming from outside the rat species—that might require adaptation and thus justify the evolution of hatred between rat clans. Indeed, one might argue that Jack's exploration of evidence from outside the text—his claim that snakes are the natural enemy of rats, which have "been fighting off snakes for probably generation upon generation"—is exactly the kind of argument that Lorenz is calling for.

So, why didn't the leaders draw the group's attention to the lines quoted in questions 2 or 7, once Jack made his claim? Why didn't they work harder to teach the discussants how to interpret the quoted lines? It is hard to say. Many factors vie for the attention of leaders of an interpretive discussion. People cannot always recall relevant passages in the text when it would be helpful to do so, despite the rounds of revision required to prepare a cluster of questions.

TONI MORRISON'S NOBEL LAUREATE SPEECH

In chapter 6, we asked, *Did the initial "evaluative" conversation help to move the group members toward the interpretive focus they eventually assumed?*

Alan and Eban have different ideas about what it means to "take responsibility." The question arises after the leader asks, "What does [the old woman] mean when she says [to the young people who visit her asking whether the bird they hold is alive or dead], 'It is your responsibility'?" (line 34). Alan maintains that the phrase means to know right from wrong. Eban asserts that it means doing what you believe is the right thing to do. Both speakers are "evaluating" the text rather than trying to interpret it.[4] Then we have Sonya:

> SONYA: I don't know … But she's [the old woman is] saying whatever the case, even … like sometimes whatever that case is, we still have the responsibility to change things. So, like, it doesn't matter what you think; … it's like believing what you think and what's for the benefit of everyone else. I don't know.

Unlike Alan and Eban, Sonya returns to the text. She focuses on the words "whatever the case" and begins to explain what the old woman may mean by them. Sonya's idea is not clear to the leader, who responds by repeating back to Sonya what she hears—"So taking responsibility is doing what is for the benefit of everyone else?" Sonya responds for a second time, "I don't know." So although Sonya has shifted focus back to the text, she has not interpreting the quoted words fully and says that she does not understand them.

These discussants, like those we observed in both groups of seventh-grade science students discussing "Rats," are unsure about how to work with the text to discover meaning in it. Although Eban, like Sonya, repeats the old woman's words, "Whatever the case," he does not try to say what she means by them. When confronted with puzzling words, Alan and Eban turn to their own experiences and ideas based on these rather than to words in the text itself.

Although she does not interpret the words she quotes fully, Sonya has made three important moves in the above excerpt—moves that open the way for the productive interpretive discussion that subsequently transpires. First, she does return to the text—the words the old woman utters and the fact that she utters them—and acknowledges that the challenge is to understand what the character means by "It is your responsibility," rather than what she, Sonya, or any other discussant might mean by them.

Second, she twice declares her own ignorance of what the old woman intends and makes no attempt to hide it. In so doing, she helps others as well as herself to recognize that ignorance of another's meaning is part of the discussion experience and is not to be shunned.

Third, while acknowledging her ignorance, Sonya begins to address it by trying to interpret other words in the text—other words that may illuminate the puzzling phrase. We saw the leader propose this very strategy in the discussions of both "Rats" and Toni Morrison's speech. Here, Sonya begins to initiate the pattern of her own accord.

Although Carl and Larry, who speak subsequently, shift the focus back to their own experiences, the group now has before it two options: (1) Each participant can try to understand the meaning of words in the text by drawing on his or her own experiences and, in effect, by arguing what the text would mean if the participant uttered those words. (2) Each participant can try to understand the meaning of puzzling words in the text by looking at the confusing text itself, and perhaps other parts of the text, more closely.

As we saw, the group selects the second option more and more frequently as the conversation continues. Although the evaluative exchanges about what it means to take responsibility were not directly related to the shared point of doubt that eventually formed, the exchanges put before the group the contrast between evaluating and interpreting, once Sonya turns the focus to text interpretation. Eventually, the discussants become more confident about pursuing close textual analysis. Let us look more closely at what happened.

Another question we asked in chapter 6: was, *How did the group move from evaluating the text to interpreting it?* Consider, for example, the following exchange about Morrison's line "Our inheritance is an affront":

SONYA: What's "an affront?"

SHG: What's "an affront"? Any ideas? Go ahead, Dave.

DAVE: I ...

SHG: Sometimes when I see a word [and] am not sure what it means, I try to read it in the context. So if you read a little bit more, let's come back, just as you were doing, Dave ... "You want us to have your old, blank eyes and see only cruelty and mediocrity."

DAVE: [It means] To think everything was, like, bad, like, see only the bad and the negative.

SHG: Okay. "You want us to have your old, blank eyes." So that sounds like what?

DAVE: To be blind like you and not be able to see ...

SHG: Be blind, be not be able to see ... So they're saying, "You want us to be like you"? Is that what you're seeing in this? [Dave nods assent.] All right, so ... what is this, "Our inheritance is an affront"?

LARRY: And is it already negative?

SHG: Already negative?

LARRY: Well, like maybe passed down negative ...

DAVE: Like, what we're getting is no good.

In contrast to the seventh-grade science students discussing "Rats," Sonya, Dave, and Larry do not flee from a puzzling passage. Sonya asks what the word "affront" means, again acknowledging her ignorance, and the leader focuses on a line that precedes it in the text: "You want us to have your old, blank eyes and see only cruelty and mediocrity." Dave and Larry work together to interpret the line, and eventually Dave illuminates the meaning of "affront" when he says, "Like, what we're getting is no good."

Compare the leader's statement "Sometimes when I see a word [and] am not sure what it means, I try to read it in the context" with the following statement that she makes in the discussion of "Rats":

> SHG: So when it says, "As-yet unknown, external selection factors are at work." Okay, remember what we're trying to do. We're trying to explain these words, and the reason we're looking at these words is because Minnie had the idea that perhaps in [the passage that contains these words], there would be some evidence that would help us to understand why these rats ... what purpose it serves for these rats to fight one another.
>
> DURANT: Rats are kinda vicious, by nature.

Here, instead of focusing the discussants on words in the "Rats" text that would help them interpret the meaning of the technical term "external selection factors," the leader directs their attention away from the text: "Okay, remember what we're trying to do." In so saying, she reminds the group why they are trying to interpret the puzzling phrase, but she does not take them to a specific place in the text to help them do it, as she does with Sonya, Larry, and Dave.

The comparison suggests that a discussion can become interpretive when the leader describes and then engages the discussants in analysis of the text. Those inexperienced with interpretive discussion must be taught how to proceed. As Sonya, Larry, and Dave worked to say no more and no less than the lines that preceded those in question, perhaps they saw what they needed to do to make progress in interpreting the puzzling phrases. And perhaps they saw that they could do it.

Return to the third question raised in chapter 6—*Why was the group successful in using textual evidence to address its shared question?* The foregoing suggests that by keeping the discussants focused on the text and showing them how to proceed in the face of puzzling words and passages, the leader taught the students how to pursue close interpretation, and they discovered the value of so doing. Consequently, they began to initiate patterns that led to a close study of Morrison's speech with one another. Look again at how Sonya draws the group's attention to line 197—a previously unexplored passage that she says she does not understand:

SONYA: "Tell us about ships turned away from shorelines at Easter, placenta in a field. Tell us about a wagonload of slaves, how they sang so softly their breath was indistinguishable from the falling snow. How they knew from the hunch of the nearest shoulder that the next stop would be their last ..."

SHG: What is happening here now?

SONYA: They're talking about how, I guess, this group of slaves, they're in like some kind of a wagon and they know that, I guess, they're going to die. I still don't get how that connects to like ... I don't know if she [Morrison] is talking about that specific generation of slaves and how they knew but they still made it, and maybe that's how she's connecting it to [lines 213–214]. Like, how they had it hard, but then their generation still survived and that they acknowledge that or they know that.

SHG: So the young people are talking to the old woman, and they say, "Tell us about ships turned away from shorelines at Easter," and so on. . . . So, in this particular passage, they seem to think she knows something or has something to tell them. Is that right? And they're trying to find out about it?

SONYA: Yes. They're asking about this specific generation of people.

SHG: Uh-huh. And they're trying to find out about them?

SONYA: About how even though they went through that, how they came out ... what was the aftermath of it?

SHG: What happened to the slaves? As though they don't know themselves and they think she does?

SONYA: Yeah.

SHG: What I'm hearing you say, Sonya, is that this [passage] is evidence or may be evidence—because we have to go through it—that the old woman comes to trust the young people because she hears them trying to learn something from her. Really asking because they don't know. Okay? It's another possibility that we could put alongside of the possibility that we've been exploring—that is, that she comes to trust them because she hears them speaking [some] truth, and [that truth], as was [stated] earlier, is that they recognize that the world's [not] so great, and as you put it, Dave, they want to do something about it and they care about it. Right?

Sonya is trying to use the text to address the question of concern to her—why the old woman comes to trust the young people by the end of the story. The student identifies and reads a passage that she thinks may provide textual evidence about the answer, and she begins to interpret the quoted lines. She does not engage in line-by-line analysis of the entire passage, but she identifies some facts that it presents, including that the young people are speaking and asking the old woman for information ("Tell us about ships turned away at Easter ... Tell us about a wagon-load of slaves").

At the same time, the leader follows some useful discussion-leading patterns, thereby exercising the productive habits of mind to help Sonya and the rest of the group.[5] To begin with, the leader asks the student directly about the meaning of the words she has read ("What is happening here now?"). In addition, she repeats back what she understands Sonya to have said ("What I'm hearing you say, Sonya, is ..."). In following the patterns, the leader is working to understand what the student intends to say and, furthermore, how the student's statements addresses the question of concern.

Finally, having repeated back Sonya's new idea, the leader contrasts it with another the group has considered—that the old woman comes to trust the young people because she hears them speaking a truth: "they recognize that the world's [not] so great, and as you put it, Dave, they want to do something about it and they care about it." In so saying, the leader positions the group as well as herself to judge which idea is best supported by the textual evidence.

Why was the group successful in using textual evidence to address its shared question? The leader tells the discussants how to proceed in the face of a puzzling passage and engages them in so doing. She also tries to understand the students' intended meanings and listens for ideas about the answer to the question of concern to them. The discussants seem to learn what to do, for they draw attention to lines in the text and work together to interpret the lines' meaning. In so doing, they come to a new idea about the answer to their question: the old woman comes to trust the young people not because she hears them trying to learn from her or speaking the truth but because she and the young people seek understanding from and with one another.[6]

Finally, one last question: *Why was the leader able to help the students by following discussion-leading patterns and, thereby, exercising useful habits of mind?* Again, we see that the preparation of a cluster of questions before the discussion helped direct the leader's listening during the discussion (see appendix D for the cluster of questions).

For example, the prepared basic question, "Does the old woman come to trust the young people because she hears them trying to learn or because she hears them speaking the truth?" suggests two ideas about the resolution. One is that the old woman hears the young people trying to learn from her, and the other is that she hears them speaking the truth. Having identified these two options, the leader was positioned to hear not only these possibilities, should the discussants pursue them, but also other options that might arise in contrast to them. As it turned out, the "open" version of the basic question became the shared point of doubt (Why did the old woman come to trust the young people?), and both options were explored in the discussion, although the group resolved in favor of neither, as described above.

Furthermore, several follow-up questions explored passages that were pursued in the discussion, so that when they were raised, the leader was familiar with them and could ponder them in relation to the question on the floor. Question 1 points to line 35 of the text, which refers to line 34: "Whatever the case, it is your responsibility"—the line that sparked the initial inquiry. Question 8 draws attention to lines 172–178, which include the sentence "Our inheritance is an affront." Question 9 explores the meaning of lines 213–215: "I trust you with the bird that is not in your hands … Look. How lovely it is, this thing that we have done—together." Having written questions about these and other passages that were discussed, the leader was better able to hear the shared point of doubt emerge in the group, follow productive discussion-leading patterns, and exercise productive habits of mind.

FINAL REFLECTION

In reflecting on the three examples of interpretive discussions presented in this book, we have addressed several questions. We have always considered the discussions with reference to the formation and resolution of a shared point of doubt—the twofold goal of an interpretive discussion. For example, the opening dialogue between Michael and the leader in the discussion of *Schoolmaster* may have helped the shared question begin to form. In the discussion of "Rats," while the first group did not raise interpretive questions because the discussants were unclear on who was doing what to whom, their progress in following ideational and interpersonal rules seemed to open a shared point of doubt for the second group. And while those discussing Toni Morrison's Nobel Laureate speech began by discussing what *they* meant by "taking responsibility" rather than what the character in the text meant by the phrase, they seemed to discover the relative power of text interpretation. They worked together to find meaning in challenging passages and, in so doing, formed a shared point of doubt and identified not one but three possible resolutions, in light of textual evidence.

Finally, the discussion-leading we have observed in the three cases was not always perfect. The coleaders of the "Rats" discussion might have helped the second group explore passages to gain insight into the meaning of "external selection factors," for example. And at some points, the attempt to repeat back what the speaker intended to say could have been more accurate.

On the other hand, the leaders' persistent call for closer textual analysis, *when that analysis was loose or not taking place at all*, seemed to help the discussants discover its usefulness. If the goal is to interpret the text, productive discussion-leading patterns often bring it about.

Using Interpretive Discussion in the Classroom

THIS BOOK HAS explored the three phases of interpretive discussion. Indeed, we have looked in detail at the preparation phase, which involves both text selection and the creation of a cluster of questions. We also explored the actual leading of the interpretive discussion by examining excerpts from three interpretive discussions. Finally, we began the reflection phase by returning to the issues raised about each discussion with respect to forming and resolving a shared point of doubt, the two-fold goal of interpretive discussion.

Yet, readers may wonder what happens when teachers integrate interpretive discussion into the curriculum. What benefits do they reap from so doing? What challenges do they face, and how do they respond to the challenges?

To continue the opportunity for reflection, I now offer some observations from educators who use interpretive discussion in their classrooms. The comments describe how teachers of English/language arts, mathematics, social studies, science, and world languages have adapted interpretive discussion to suit their pedagogical situations. The comments come from teachers at the elementary, middle, and secondary grade levels. They speak of advantages that accrue from interpretive discussion and related activities. They also discuss challenges they have faced, together with strategies they have found helpful in overcoming the challenges.[1]

Let us begin with some reasons teachers give for using interpretive discussion with their students. First, a story from Nela, a social studies teacher who has been working in a suburban high school classroom for more than ten years and who uses interpretive discussion to help students tackle primary source documents:[2]

> NELA: [In my Advanced Placement] U.S. history class, the first [text that we use is] the Declaration of Independence. What I notice right off the bat is that kids ... will ask a question about how this [document] has affected American history or something like that. They think they're getting deep, but what they don't understand is that we want them to get more into the meaning of text.
>
> So the second time, we do a full-length interpretive discussion about the Gettysburg Address—again, a short text. But it does take a lot of reminding for the students to bring [out] what Lincoln was saying in those words. Often they want to talk about the war, or they'll talk about race relations, or what the Confederacy really meant to Lincoln, or something like that.
>
> I really want to build the kids' critical reading skills, and I think after those sessions, they understand that it is vitally important to just trust the reading of something, even though it seems like a very familiar text—everybody knows the Declaration of Independence.

Nela sounds much like Lindsay, the high school English teacher from whom we heard at the beginning of the introduction. Both are eager for students to learn to interpret the words of the text for themselves. Thus, it is insufficient, Nela says, to relate what the text says to events not mentioned in the text (e.g., historical events). Instead, students need to grapple with what the text says and means, much as they have done in the cases explored throughout the book. Learning to trust and care for your own ideas about the meaning of a text and, indeed, about what others say is a profound benefit of participation in interpretive discussion.

Megan, a high school mathematics teacher, has been teaching in an urban school for two and one-half years. In one respect, her voice sounds like Nela's:

> MEGAN: I try to give the students problems where you can have multiple approaches. And I want them to explain what they did to solve the problem. I want them to explain, "Well, I tried this number, and I found out my answer was too small so

then I changed my number and I did this" … I want them to understand the process that they went through. I'm hoping that translates to what we do in class to help our discussion. So that when we address something new in class, they can be like, "I was thinking this, and this is why."

I think we learn math to be able to solve [mathematics] problems, but we can learn how to solve other things as well.

When Megan says, "I want them to explain what they did to solve the problem," she tells us that the text before the students is their own thinking about the mathematics problem—a problem that can be solved in more than one way. Where the text is a person's own thinking about an object, the respondent must explain the thinking in terms of the intentions, actions, observed consequences, subsequent reasoning, and subsequent actions. Likewise, when a discussant selects a passage from the Declaration of Independence and tries to say no more and no less than what the quoted words say, he or she tries to explain the intentions, actions, consequences, and subsequent reasoning of that text. In both cases, the person creates an interpretation. Megan, a mathematics teacher, like Nela, a social studies teacher, and Lindsay, the English teacher, wants her students to be able to interpret texts for themselves. Furthermore, she believes that students learn problem-solving strategies that apply beyond the realm of mathematics.

Kirsten, a fourth-grade teacher of social studies, mathematics, language arts, and science, talks of her experience using interpretive discussion across disciplines:

KIRSTEN: I would say that it [interpretive discussion] is pretty similar in social studies and in reading, because a lot of that is based on [verbal] text. In science, it's more they have to come up with the evidence based on their investigations or experiments with things.

For example, in geology, [we look at objects and ask], Which of these are rocks? Which of these contain this specific mineral? So again, it's really asking, What is the evidence for your claim? They really have to analyze the evidence that they've received and see which claim it supports.

In science, so much of it is looking beyond the obvious. In one [lesson], we looked for the presence of calcite, which forms bubbles when it's submerged in acid, so [we tried placing rocks] in vinegar. But the rocks, when you put them in [the vinegar], also release bubbles from the air that were trapped under the rock. So [the students] really have to look for the presence of a specific type of bubble when testing for calcite. They are analyzing the information that they're collecting.

And I can definitely see that another type of text is responding to math problems and explaining math answers and [your] reasoning.

As Kirsten points out, different disciplines draw on different kinds of texts. English and social studies, for example, often focus interpretation upon verbal objects—books, articles, poems, historical documents, or textbook material. However, like Megan, the high school mathematics teacher, Kirsten sees that a person's thinking about a mathematics problem is a kind of text that can be interpreted. In science, the text is not necessarily verbal, as is the case when rocks are submerged in vinegar, and the text is a phenomenon created by doing particular things to objects.

Yet, regardless of its material composition, interpretive discussion treats the text as an object that has meaning. The nature of that meaning is, by definition, something that is unclear to those who contemplate it. This is why participants have a discussion, or work together to try to understand it. As Kirsten argues, their work involves collecting information about the object and "analyzing" it. The work always involves "finding evidence for one's claim" about the meaning of the object.

Given what she says, it may be that the students in Kirsten's fourth-grade classroom are working with subject matter in reading, social studies, language arts, science, and mathematics to meet both of the Common Core State Standards mentioned in the introduction. That is, they may be learning to interpret the texts and engage in collaborative discussions with their peers when studying all of these subjects. If that is the case, one suspects that Kirsten has discovered how to use interpretive discussion and related activities to make her curriculum consistent and coherent.

Finally, a story about the power of interpretive discussion from Jasmine, a teacher of high school Spanish in an urban school. She describes her experience leading a discussion about a piece of art titled "Skeletons":

> JASMINE: I wasn't sure how it was going to go, because my students weren't really exposed to a ton of art. But it actually ended up being pretty successful to the point where students did come to a common understanding and then took it one step further—which isn't like pure interpretive discussion. It was more evaluative, where at the end, when they come to a common understanding of the text, they related it to their own lives. I feel like they were able to share aspects of their lives that they otherwise wouldn't have been able to do because they felt comfortable since everybody

had a common understanding of the text. So it was very interesting to me how the interpretive discussion helped them to evaluate and helped them deal with a tough situation in their experience.

Jasmine does not describe the personal problem that concerned the students. Once the interpretive portion of the conversation came to an end or even, perhaps, along the way, the group stopped interpreting "Skeletons" and began discussing implications of the conversation for the resolution of a dilemma that for them existed outside the text. In other words, they took up evaluative dialogue.[3] According to Jasmine, that dialogue was satisfying and productive. That it occurred suggests both that the group members had come to care about and trust one another and that the interpretation of "Skeletons" may have given them ideas about the resolution of their shared personal problem.

Although teachers of many subjects and grade levels attest to the power and benefits of interpretive discussion, some acknowledge that they face challenges working with the pedagogy. In what follows, teachers speak about the challenges and their efforts to address them.

THE CHALLENGE OF TIME

Dedre, a middle school language arts teacher (fifth and eighth grades) of more than ten years' experience, has served as a mentor for student teachers over the years. She talks about the importance of patience:

> **DEDRE:** I say to my student teachers: be patient with interpretive discussion. It isn't the kind of thing where you say, "Here's the expectation for this lesson, and here's the rubric, and let's get going." It doesn't happen that way. [The students] need to understand the goal we want to achieve and what they get out of it.
>
> I start teaching in August. By October, the class has gone through this [had interpretive discussions] about three or four times. By then, I feel that we're all excited about it—we're all engaged in it. We're all learning from it. Along the way, between August and October, we are tweaking it in our class.
>
> When I did interpretive discussion with the fifth graders, they were all about to jump into having the discussion, and we realized that was not what we wanted to do—to just have everybody talking, just talking. No, it's about building on each other; it's about using the text. It's about referencing what somebody else said, connecting it to

the text, and then making this a deeper discussion, and all of that from fifth graders takes time and patience.

Many teachers find that it takes students time to understand the value of interpretive discussion and the activities related to it. Indeed, students may need to experience these discussions and related activities multiple times before they know what to do and feel their benefit. Both teacher and student must accept that immediate satisfaction may not occur.

Janeen, a high school English teacher in a suburban school for more than five years, describes another challenge of time: "You know, I must admit that in the last couple of years, I have not been able to write the basic question with the eight follow-up questions in the format that we were [taught to use]. I just have not had that type of time for the text."

Yes, developing clusters of questions takes time. Teachers address the challenge in various ways. "When I do the interpretive discussion," says Janeen, "if we're doing *Frankenstein*, I will lead a discussion on just a section of it. Or if we're doing *Notes from Underground* [I might lead a discussion on], part 10 of the first section. So the discussion wouldn't necessarily be on the text as a whole. One of the ways to make it less challenging in terms of time is to really focus on a small section."

Whether the text is one page or one hundred pages, the preparation is the same: a basic question plus eight follow-up questions (see chapter 2). Still, a shorter text allows more time for question development, as the amount of reading is smaller.

As another suggestion, Dedre recalls preparing questions for the short story "The Most Dangerous Game," by Richard Kennel, with her fellow teacher: "We happened to be using the same text. I'd been leading discussion about it for two or three years, and I wanted to make sure I was using questions that were still [points of doubt for me]. I wanted a fresh pair of eyes."

The two teachers met to share and refine their questions. In so doing, they may have discovered that they shared a point of doubt or that they no longer cared about a question that had previously concerned them. If a shared point of doubt is reached, the two can develop follow-up questions together and perhaps save time forming queries that meet the criteria of clarity (see the sidebar "Summary of Criteria for a Clear Cluster of Questions" in appendix A).

Another suggestion made by Dedre and others is to engage the students in forming the cluster of questions:

DEDRE: I ask the kids to bring their own questions [about the meaning of the text]. I usually find that when the kids and I are developing the questions together, I didn't necessarily need another teacher.

One of the reasons I love doing it with the kids is each set of students brings a new perspective to the text. I walk away every time, even when I've done *The Most Dangerous Game*, which is one of my favorite texts, several times over the last decade—each time, I can tell you without hesitation, I walked away learning something. And that's why teaching has been so amazing for me: I walk away learning something every day.

Dedre comes to the class with questions she had written about the text, but she does not come with a prepared cluster. Indeed, the students, who also come with questions, work with the teacher to develop a shared point of doubt. As a consequence, Dedre experiences the joy of learning new things from continued study of the text.

Miriam, a fifth-grade teacher who works with "lower track" students in an urban public school, has been teaching for more than five years. She, too, develops questions with her students: "Many times we will go right into something. For example, we read a really awesome book called *Freak the Mighty*, a lovely novel, which is above their level and so I read it to them and they read along. We spent so much time in that novel just stopping and sort of hopping into the psyche of the characters. So in that case, there was nothing prepared. The questions arose spontaneously out of their curiosity."

Miriam explains that while she herself has read the book before, she has not taken the time to prepare a cluster of questions about its meaning. As she reads to the students, they will raise questions trying to figure out things in the story about which they were unclear. In our interview, Miriam suddenly stops herself. "The story is about two very, very complex main characters," she says. "Now that I'm saying this out loud, should I do an interpretive discussion with it now? Wow! I think that would actually be awesome."

Once Miriam finishes reading the story to the students, she can develop a cluster of questions around a question that they had been struggling to resolve. Or, she can work with them to develop a cluster. She might say, "Okay, this question—we've been raising it throughout the story, and now we're all finished reading. Let's go back and look at some of the different places in the text where there might be something that happens, or the characters might do something that could help us think about that problem some more."

Since the students in Miriam's class have been raising questions as the reading proceeded, they may be in a position to identify a shared point of doubt—a candidate for the basic question of a cluster of questions. Indeed, the above description of classroom activity mirrors the first step of cluster development described in chapter 3—the spontaneous raising of questions as one reads. The subsequent steps of returning to the text, identifying passages that help address a point of doubt, and interpreting them, seem to follow naturally.

Jason, the eighth-grade language arts teacher we met in the introduction, has been working in an urban school when the interview takes place. He tells us that before discussing a text, he and his students prepare questions that they share with one another:

> JASON: Now, I always have my questions prepared, okay? And [the students] come in with questions. And I will have a theme that they have to align their [questions] with. It won't be hard for them to do that, because the theme is overarching. As an example, I held interpretive discussions about Elie Wiesel's *Night*. So for one section, I said, "Okay, our theme for this week's reading is the dehumanization of the people in the concentration camps. Now, I want you to [raise questions] dealing with this idea of dehumanization." So, I might have some questions that I want to broach, but I'm also asking them for questions that are related to the theme.

In preparing to lead an interpretive discussion, Jason writes questions about some section of a text—questions related to a theme that he wants to explore with students. Similarly, the students come to the discussion having read the assigned section and written questions about passages that pertain to the theme. They are ready to work together identifying a shared point of doubt and developing follow-up questions. Perhaps that point of doubt will relate to the theme that the teacher has identified. Here, the task of developing a cluster of questions becomes a joint project.

Teachers may struggle to find the time for adequate discussion preparation. However, the answer is not to eliminate the preparation of a cluster of questions. The comments from Janeen, Dedre, Miriam, and Jason suggest that when preparation is shared with colleagues and students (and the sharing can be done in a variety of ways), the preparation can become a meaningful learning activity for all and may save the teacher time clarifying questions by himself or herself prior to the discussion.

Sadie, an English teacher who has been teaching in an urban high school for more than five years, offers a third challenge of time:

> SADIE: I found, with revising the questions, that it was very challenging when I was working with them at the beginning, to give feedback to five classes of twenty-five students, in a timely manner. Because I wanted to spend a healthy amount of time with them helping them to revise [the questions to clarify them], so I would always feel pressured that I would have to [collect their written questions and return them to the students] the next day. And that was just a lot. So, I have to think of a way where I'm not trying to revise a hundred and fifty student questions.

I suggested to Sadie that she ask students to help one another revise their questions. In doing so, a leader could distribute the list of the criteria for evaluating a cluster of questions and then discuss them (see the sidebar "Summary of Criteria for a Clear Cluster of Questions" in appendix A). The leader might introduce the criteria slowly, so that gradually, the students learn what each criterion means and when to apply it. If they are revising questions that are not part of a cluster, for example, they will focus particularly on criteria 2, 3, and 4. That is, the questions should be interpretive (criterion 2), should be free of technical terms and vague phrases (criterion 3), and should quote and fully interpret passages that help pose the question and suggest possible resolution (criterion 4).

Once students learn the criteria that a clear question needs to meet, they will be able to assist one another in clarifying questions and, eventually, entire clusters. Thus, the burden of time is reduced for the teacher, and the students are acquiring higher and higher standards of clarity.

FINDING APPROPRIATE TEXTS IN MATHEMATICS AND SCIENCE

An ongoing adventure for all teachers who wish to engage their students in interpretive discussion is the identification of discussable texts—texts with enough ambiguity in them to sustain at least forty-five minutes of conversation about their meaning. Teachers of English/language arts and social studies may have less difficulty finding a suitable text than those teaching mathematics and science.

Megan, the high school mathematics teacher who makes texts out of student thinking about mathematical problems, describes another source of discussable mathematical texts:

> MEGAN: I've found some short articles about math in the *New York Times*. And for those, I had students actually read the article for homework. They [were asked] to come to school with questions [about its meaning] so that we could discuss it. They are short articles, written in a nice and friendly manner so that you can understand them even without much of a math background. And generally, the articles have great pictures and diagrams.
>
> These articles go along with something that we're studying. For example, one was talking about different kinds of infinity. We were studying this topic in discrete [mathematics], and we were talking about the different sizes of the infinity. The article did a great job of explaining infinity in one way, and we'd already talked about it a lot in class. Some of the students seemed like they were kind of understanding [the concept]. But some of them definitely weren't convinced. So it was interesting to see how those two types of students approached the article and the questions they asked about it because of where they were.

In Megan's classroom, the text includes the mathematical thinking in newspaper articles. Not only is the meaning of the article discussed, but through interpretive discussion, the meaning found there is also related to additional texts—the students' thinking about the topic of infinity, perhaps a discussion of it presented in a textbook, or students' thinking about the relations between texts. In effect, Megan builds discussable texts in her classes by bringing together materials that present mathematical perspectives on particular topics.

Adam, a high school science teacher who has been working in an urban school for more than five years, talks about the importance of breaking down texts into more manageable portions:

> ADAM: I conduct interpretive discussions of short sections of text in my class all the time. I do this as a group activity to ensure that students understand the text and, in

particular, understand the definitions of all the words in the text. It's also a great way to assess reading level in order to guide learning strategy.

I have a classroom set of books, and so I'll hand out the books and I will identify important sections—particularly introductory sections where it kind of summarizes things. We'll read the text and discuss words that they may not know, and make sure that they have an understanding of the scientific vocabulary.

These "interpretive discussions of short sections of the text" sound like those about which Adam himself does not have questions. Instead, he is allowing the students to raise issues, perhaps related to the meaning of words, that he plans to answer. But he continues:

> **ADAM:** One of the things that we were covering today in my earth science classes is continental drift. The idea was proposed in the early part of the twentieth century. It wasn't until the 1960s that it was really accepted. Why would someone question that the continents just plowed through the oceans? And so we had a discussion about the objections. And there were some very serious objections because [initially], it was just an idea that had no proof.

When Adam says that the class discussed why people objected to the theory of continental drift, it sounds as though he, as well as the students, may have been unclear about the reasoning of those who had reservations about the theory. Does Adam engage his students in reflecting on issues that may be resolved in more than one way, given the evidence? And if so, how can he find ambiguity and multiple perspectives in textbooks, which by definition attempt to present a factual and unambiguous perspective?

> **ADAM:** In another class, we're addressing the pros and cons of nuclear energy, because we're studying nuclear chemistry right now. One [text] is a *Wall Street Journal* article, and another text is a summary that I came up with that [was] taken from several articles. Both texts are two-sided, so you know it's the kind of thing that you can have them read one day and have the discussion the next day. And whenever I do this, they just love it. They love it.

Adam, like Megan, suggests juxtaposing texts to help students entertain a variety of perspectives on topics. The different perspectives enable the students to relate to the topic and indeed to the texts themselves by seeing that taken together, the various viewpoints suggest more than one resolution. Evidently, some questions that have emerged in his classes might be ones for which Adam does not have a certain answer. These questions may be raised by the students or the teacher, since all have access to multiple perspectives. Maybe Adam's students enjoy the discussions because the questions have been addressed in more than one way, and the students enjoy thinking about the answers in light of their study of multiple sources.

REVISING STUDENT EXPECTATIONS OF THE SCHOOL EXPERIENCE

Some teachers indicated that student expectations sometimes made it difficult for the students to embrace the opportunities offered by interpretive discussion and related activities, at least at first. Teachers mentioned the following challenges in student attitude:

- Students are more comfortable addressing questions that have a right answer or that can be addressed with reference to personal experience rather than interpreting the text.
- Students have difficulty and lose patience with the task of interpreting passages fully.
- Students do not always build sound arguments in which they relate passages they have interpreted to the resolution of their points of doubt.

How have teachers addressed these attitudinal challenges? Let's consider them one by one.

Discomfort with Interpretive Questions

Miriam, the fifth-grade urban teacher, describes the challenge of students' preference for factual over interpretive questions:

> MIRIAM: One of the biggest challenges I have is that we track our students at our school. And I actually teach what's called the lower track—the "mainstreamed" track. Because of that, a lot of my readers are right about the second-grade [reading] level. These are not special-ed students. They just for whatever reason have managed to slip through reading at a second-grade level. They've spent so long not understanding

what they read that they lack confidence. And so they're very comfortable with [factual questions]: What color was the sky? It was blue. Who was the boyfriend? It was Doug.[4] But when we get to deepest point-of-doubt [interpretive] questions, it's such a leap for them. They don't know how to answer a question that doesn't have a right or a wrong answer.

The situation that Miriam describes is not easy for a teacher to ameliorate. How does she encourage students to raise or address interpretive questions if they are hesitant to speak unless they know the "right" answer? Miriam describes her approach:

MIRIAM: At the beginning of the year, I use all kinds of interpretive discussion ideas and approaches in my actual teaching. Let's say we read a short story. I might pose one or two questions and then have them work with a small group to come up with a question or two. And it has to be a question that seems to be resolved in more than one way, given what the text says. So I get them into [drawing] inferences: "What does this mean?" I push them that way. We're actually getting to the point right now where we're going to be moving into literature circles and doing interpretive discussion on *Number the Stars*—it's our social-responsibility unit. And I really feel that at this point, my kids are going to be able to handle it. So scaffolding them instructionally and making sure I'm questioning and that they're constantly questioning—that's what I do.

Miriam takes a long-term approach with her students. In a variety of contexts, she poses interpretive questions and asks the students to work together to form additional such questions. Over time, these opportunities help students understand how posing and responding to interpretive queries feels—and feels different from asking and answering questions that have right or expected answers. Eventually, the students are ready to speak in an interpretive discussion, she says.

Caroline, who leads a combined fourth- and fifth-grade class in a suburban setting, speaks not of students who prefer to answer factual questions but of those who prefer evaluative questions: "I have found it challenging to take students from the experienced-based discussion, where prior knowledge and connections dictate the conversations, to a text-based discussion."

What is an "experience-based discussion"? Perhaps we saw an example when the high school seniors at the Canterbury School begin to explain what the old woman in Toni Morrison's story means by "taking responsibility." Instead of trying to interpret what the old woman means by the term, the students discuss what they themselves mean by it. In other words, they use criteria gleaned from their personal experiences. Caroline continues with another example:

CAROLINE: I started this year exploring the ideas of good and evil. My co-teacher and I chose to read *Beowulf,* Native American folk tales, and excerpts from *Harry Potter.* Since good and evil is something that students can relate to in their lives, initially we found—even though we had them craft interpretive questions before the discussions—we found that they would say, "Oh yeah, this reminds me of so-and-so in second grade who did this, and they were evil or good because ..." I think there is a value to that. But by offering up their own experiences and things that they had seen, they were creating this common understanding of what good and evil was. Yet, I had chosen the texts to offer them insights into what good can be and evil can be. So essentially, the experience-based discussions weren't getting them to new knowledge.

The text-based discussions are where they are looking at the words that are actually in the text, quoting from it, and then offering up what has morphed into what we are now calling a "question of possibility." When they asked the question of possibility, they let the text allow them to reach a new but common understanding of whatever it is.

While Caroline sees value in allowing students to answer questions like "What is good?" or "What is evil" by drawing on their personal experiences, she wants them to have new ideas about the meaning of these terms. The "question of possibility" she speaks of seems to be one for which there are different possible resolutions, depending on the textual evidence. Thus, instead of defining "good" and "evil" by coming to a consensus based on personal experience, the students explore the text to develop questions that identify new possibilities that perhaps none in the group had imagined previously. Caroline continues:

One thing that I do to facilitate [the students'] understanding of the difference between an experienced-based and a text-based discussion is videotape their discussions and then ask them to reflect on [what they see in the video]. They write down the types of things that people were saying. Then we sort the things that people say into different categories. I ask them what comments or questions helped give them a new idea about good or evil. All of the [comments] that helped them get to a new idea were the more interpretive, text-based comments or questions.

Videotaping student discussions and asking students to separate new ideas from others might sound time-consuming. Caroline was asked if it was worth the time:

> **CAROLINE:** It took a lot of time and reflection, including conversations with my co-teacher, to realize that that [videotaping and analyzing the discussions] is a necessary step for [the students]. But it was so worth it that I will absolutely take that time every single year from here on out. It has really set the tone for our year, the fact that we started with the heavy emphasis on interpretive discussion. And now they have written a position paper—or an expository paper, if you will—about good and evil. They got their information from these texts and from the discussion and from challenging each other. And it has been essential in developing critical thinking, this reading and looking very closely at the text. It's been phenomenal.

Thus, although initially resistant to close text interpretation, Caroline's students may have had a change of heart. Instead of preferring to address questions with reference to prior, personal experiences, they may now understand the payoff of working to grasp what the text before them intends to say, as well as what others in the discussion say. The payoff is new and perhaps better ideas about the answers to the questions.

Difficulty Interpreting Passages Fully

Some teachers indicate that because their students have difficulty interpreting quoted words fully, they initially resist it. Indeed, precise interpretation is difficult, and even for scholars, it remains a challenge. Yet, like the social studies teacher Nela, many teachers maintain that their students do make progress with the task. Jason, the eighth-grade language arts teacher, found that a writing activity helped the students persist with careful text interpretation:

> **JASON:** I just finished *Romeo and Juliet* with my students. Their final project was to put Capulet, the Nurse, Friar Lawrence, and the state on trial for the death of Romeo and Juliet. And admissible evidence? It had to be pieces of text. And they had to go really line by line and word by word and make the link [from passages in the text] to either their guilt or their innocence.

Jason indicates that "trying" some characters for the deaths of Romeo and Juliet by quoting and interpreting passages that give evidence of their guilt or innocence requires the students to take the three steps of argument construction outlined in chapter 4.

First, in writing their essays, the students identify relevant textual evidence. Second, in support of their claims about guilt or innocence, they interpret the evidence by "going line by line and word by word." Third, the students must explain why the quoted words, as understood, support the claim.

Jason's students must execute, in writing, the steps of argument formation that they have learned to follow in discussion. And interpreting the evidence fully receives particular attention here. You can imagine how such an activity would show the students how patient, detailed interpretation helps make their arguments persuasive.

Failure to Build Sound Arguments Based on Textual Evidence

Laila, a high school English teacher during her first year of teaching, uses *Of Mice and Men* as an example of encouraging the students to form sound arguments based on the text:

> LAILA: Let's say the student is trying to find some passage that supports the point that Curly's wife is a bully. We might start with, "Okay, do you know what you're looking for?" So a kid might say something like, "Well, it was that part where Curly's wife was hanging out with George and Lenny in the barn." So now we're getting to where in the book that happened: "Okay, was that at the beginning, middle, or end? How can we narrow down where we're looking in the book (that you're not allowed to write in!), where to find that part, that little scene?" So I say, "Can you actually now find it? Go find it." Now they're drilling down to whatever piece from the book is helping them support their point. Sometimes they'll get to the right scene and pick a quote that's just not the right one. So I ask, "Does that prove what you're trying to prove? Okay, let's find something else. Like, pretend you're a lawyer. You are trying to prove to me that this woman is a bully. I need some good evidence. Find something better."

Like Caroline and Miriam, Laila guides her students through steps that will help them meet the goals of interpretive discussion. Here, the task is to support a claim using textual evidence. Since the students are not allowed to write in the book, they will need to recall the location of relevant evidence—not always an easy task with a long work.

To help them develop the patience needed, Laila first asks for the location of the relevant scene and then the relevant passage within the scene. Occasionally, the student reads the passage, interprets it, and having done so, acknowledges that it does not support the claim after all. Thus, the steps are repeated, perhaps now aimed at identifying a new passage that provides more convincing evidence. Learning how to look for new scenes or lines within scenes helps a reader develop the patience needed to find relevant evidence and develop sound arguments that support claims.

THE CHALLENGE OF ASSESSMENT

How does the teacher determine what students gain from participating in interpretive discussion? Dedre, the suburban eighth-grade language arts teacher, comments as follows:

> DEDRE: The interpretive discussion in my classroom may take three days, so there are multiple ways that I assess what students learn from it. First, I have them read the text and annotate it. So, I collect the text after the discussion with their annotations in order to understand what kind of thinking has been going on in their heads.
>
> Second, when it comes to the discussion, I have a rubric. The participant gets one point for making a comment, two points for asking a question, three points for adding on to a point brought up by someone else, and four points for raising a question or idea no one has yet mentioned. Then, [the participant] gets four points if the question or comment becomes the introduction into a new line of thinking. Through all of that, they have to reference the text. They get zero points if they fail to reference the text.
>
> Finally, I ask participants to take one of the questions that we discussed as a group and write their response to it using text examples and discussion examples. So, they could be taking notes during discussion about what someone said that they thought was valuable.

The three-pronged approach to assessment described above is but one suggestion. In presenting it, I am not urging its adoption. Rather, I hope that readers will think about the skills and habits of mind that are of value and will design assessment around these.

In Dedre's classroom, she is, first of all, interested in the students' thoughtful reflection while they are reading. Thus, she reviews the comments and questions that students write in the text while they are reading. Where writing in the text is not allowed, a teacher could ask the discussants to jot down on a separate paper or type on a computer the questions that come up while they read. Perusing those could provide the teacher with comparable data.

Likewise, Dedre's point system for student contributions values those that respond to or add to the comments and questions of others, offer a new idea, and open a new line of investigation, for example. Some readers might quibble with the point distribution or the idea of a point system altogether. But are all contributions to discussion equally valuable? Discussion leaders must answer this question to create an adequate rubric or another form of discussion assessment.

Finally, like Jason, Dedre asks her students to prepare a written response to a question discussed by the group. Such a request may be inappropriate for some subjects and grade levels. First- and second-grade students, for example, may have difficulty writing down their ideas. Likewise, thinking about mathematical issues may be best communicated through computational steps in addition to or instead of verbal commentary. At the same time, the opportunity to collect one's thoughts about a shared point of doubt and express these in the form of a coherent argument supported by textual evidence may show both student and teacher a lot about what has been learned from the discussion.

Interpretive discussion can be challenging for students and teachers alike. It is not easy to become a rigorous thinker, a perceptive listener, or an effective leader. But despite the challenges, students and teachers across the country are doing it— in language arts, social studies, mathematics, science, world languages, and other disciplines, and at the elementary, middle, and secondary school levels.

LAST WORDS

This book has explored the three phases of interpretive discussion, namely, preparation, leading, and reflection. I have tried to describe each of these phases and the practices, skills, and habits of mind that can help leaders and discussants achieve the goals of each phase.

Thus, after introducing the three phases (chapter 1), we explored such topics as picking a suitable text for discussion (chapter 2) and developing a cluster of questions prior to the discussion (chapter 3). Then, we looked at excerpts from three interpretive discussions. In the first discussion, a group of high school sophomores discuss the poem *Schoolmaster*, by Yevgeny Yevtushenko (chapter 4). In the second, two groups of seventh-grade science students discuss a scientific analysis, "Rats," by Konrad Lorenz (chapter 5). The third discussion involved a group of high-school seniors discussing Toni Morrison's Nobel Laureate lecture of 1993 (chapter 6). We then further reflected on the three discussions, addressing questions that had been raised about each (chapter 7).

In perusing the discussions, chapter 7 looked at two fundamental questions that arise during the reflection phase. First, does the group come to a shared point of doubt about the meaning of the text—a question that most if not all discussants wish to resolve? And second, does the group make progress toward resolution by developing arguments to support claims based on textual evidence? Some of the groups made more progress toward these goals than did others. And we have seen why that was the case in each instance.

The aim of this book is to encourage readers to undertake interpretive discussion with their students. As the teachers who were highlighted in this conclusion attest, there are great rewards to be reaped, despite the challenges. Furthermore, the challenges can be addressed, as the teachers explain. Indeed, facing the challenges often helps leaders to develop the skills and resources needed to effectively lead interpretive discussion.

For example, by helping students to discover that the discussion is more satisfying if they work to interpret one passage fully than if they partially interpret several passages, the leaders themselves learn to say no more and no less than what the quoted words say. By developing a cluster of questions with students or another colleague, leaders acquire the skills of questioning and listening to understand what another intends to say. They also become increasingly better at detecting ambiguity in the text and in what is heard and thus develop higher standards of clarity. Finding and creating discussable texts helps leaders learn to detect ambiguity and identify sources of possible resolution. Videotaping discussions to see the outcomes of evaluating rather than interpreting a text helps viewers judge the persuasiveness of each kind of argument. It also helps them see how individuals in the group are working to help one another with the tasks at hand. And perusing student reflections on the questions that have been discussed builds leaders' understanding of what makes a good argument.

So, now the ball is in the reader's court. In several chapters, I mentioned information given in appendixes A, B, E, and F. You may duplicate and distribute this material to leaders and participants. These appendixes provide orientation to the different phases of interpretive discussion and will draw people into the activities involved. Included are appendix A, "Overview: Preparing to Lead Interpretive Discussion"; appendix B, "Overview: Leading Interpretive Discussion"; appendix E, "The Nature of Questions"; and appendix F, "Overview: Preparing to Participate in Interpretive Discussion."

Best of luck, and enjoy the challenges, excitement, and learning through interpretive discussion!

Overview: Preparing to Lead Interpretive Discussion

THE GOAL OF the preparation phase is to select a text for discussion and to prepare a cluster of questions about its meaning. Let's look at these two steps. When done well, these two steps can encourage a productive interpretive discussion.

SELECTING A TEXT

The text for an interpretive discussion could be a book, a film, a set of data, a mathematics problem, a painting, or an artifact of some sort. It can be any object, delimited in some way, whose ambiguity permits you to write a *cluster of questions* (defined below) about its meaning. However, a discussable text is not necessarily a suitable text. The suitability of the text depends on the circumstances of the discussion and the purposes of the leader-teacher. For example, to determine suitability, you might consider (1) the age of the discussants, (2) their prior experience with interpretive discussion, (3) the subject matter of the text, (4) the length of the text, (5) the time available for the discussion, and (6) the interests of the discussants. The text selected should be suitable as well as discussable.[1]

PREPARING A CLUSTER OF QUESTIONS

To prepare yourself to lead an interpretive discussion, you need to develop a cluster of questions about the meaning of the text that you select. I borrow the phrase "cluster of questions" from *Shared Inquiry Handbook: A Basic Guide for Discussion Leaders and Participants*.[2] The cluster includes a basic question, which expresses the deepest point of doubt that you have about the meaning of the text—the question that you wish most to resolve. In addition to the basic question, you also need to write eight follow-up questions, which are included in the cluster. The follow-up questions, like the basic question, are interpretive. In addition, they point to passages that, if interpreted in at least one way, suggest ideas about the resolution of the basic question. To develop a cluster of questions, I recommend that you do the following:

1. Read or study the text, and write questions about its meaning as you do so. Number the questions, noting page numbers or other locations to which they refer. Peruse the text again, adding questions if more occur to you.

2. Review your questions. If some are factual or evaluative, set these aside. Looking at your interpretive questions, decide if some relate to others and if there are one or two issues about the meaning of the text that you might care to resolve. Perhaps your deepest point of doubt—the question you wish most to resolve—has not been posed directly or clearly yet. Your goal in developing the cluster is to identify this basic question and to write eight more clear interpretive questions that, if resolved in at least one way, suggest ideas for resolving the basic question. The deepest point of doubt will become your basic question, and the additional questions will become follow-up questions.

3. If you are coleading the discussion, meet with your coleader. Read through the interpretive questions of interest to each of you. Ask each other about the meaning of the questions that both of you have written, searching for technical terms and vague, ambiguous phrases. Replace these words with words that express intended meaning. If you are leading by yourself, pursue the same activities alone.

4. If coleading, work with your partner to find a shared concern—a question that both of you wish to resolve about the meaning of the text. The question may be other than those you have written thus far. Pose the shared concern as clearly as possible. While working, consult the sidebar "Summary of Criteria for a Clear

Cluster of Questions" at the end of this appendix to understand the standards of clarity that all questions in the cluster need to meet. If leading by yourself, pursue the same activities alone.

5. Once you have clarified your (shared) deepest point of doubt, which becomes the basic question, your next task is to write eight follow-up questions that explore its resolution. Each question should refer to a different, specific place in the text that you quote and interpret fully. The entire cluster should meet the eight standards of clarity presented in the sidebar "Summary of Criteria for a Clear Cluster of Questions" at the end of this appendix. (See appendixes C and D for examples of texts and clusters of questions that aim to meet the standards of clarity.)

6. Having written the basic question and eight follow-up questions, read all the way through the draft of the cluster. Try to identify the deepest point of doubt. Is it stated in the basic question? Or is it suggested in one or more follow-up questions but not yet stated by the basic question? Does there seem to be more than one deepest point of doubt? Revise the basic question and the follow-up questions as needed, applying the eight criteria for a clear cluster of questions presented in the sidebar "Summary of Criteria for a Clear Cluster of Questions" until the cluster meets all the criteria.

Notes

1. This handout refers to Sophie Haroutunian-Gordon's *Interpretive Discussion: Engaging Students in Text-Based Conversations* (Cambridge, MA: Harvard Education Press, 2014), chapter 2, which contains a detailed discussion of text selection, and chapter 3, which explains criteria for a clear cluster of questions.
2. Donald H. Whitfield and Daniel Born, eds., *Shared Inquiry Handbook: A Basic Guide for Discussion Leaders and Participants* (Chicago: Great Books Foundation, 2007).

SUMMARY OF CRITERIA FOR
A CLEAR CLUSTER OF QUESTIONS

1. The cluster consists of a basic question and at least eight follow-up questions.

2. All questions are interpretive.

3. All questions are clear.

4. The follow-up questions quote and fully interpret passages in the text, indicating the locations in the text precisely.

5. The basic question expresses the deepest point of doubt.

6. All follow-up questions suggest ideas about the resolution of the basic question.

7. The basic question is in the proper form, indicating the questioner's best guess about the resolution.

8. All questions express points of doubt as concisely as possible.

Overview: Leading Interpretive Discussion

A GOOD INTERPRETIVE DISCUSSION is one in which the participants come to a shared concern—a question that they cannot yet answer, but wish to answer, about the meaning of the text—and make progress toward its resolution. Let us look at key features of an interpretive discussion.[1]

THE NATURE OF THE CONVERSATION

The goal of the discussion is twofold:

1. Identify the shared question and clarify it until it contains no vague phrases or technical terms (words that could mean more than one thing or whose intended meaning is unclear).
2. Address the shared question by suggesting resolutions that seem to be supported by evidence in the text—specific passages or places that they identify in the text.

In working toward the twofold goal, discussants need to:

- Fully interpret the cited passages and explain how their interpretations support the suggested resolutions.
- Evaluate the strength of the arguments in support of the suggested resolutions.

As they engage in these activities, group members will question one another about the meaning of things that are said, in the text and by one another, so that the passages in the text become fully interpreted and sound arguments are developed in support of the claims.

THE ROLE OF THE LEADER

To help discussants form and pursue the resolution of a shared concern, the leader needs to:

1. Be very familiar with the text. Preparing the cluster of questions and revising it requires you to explore the text in great depth. By doing so, you will find it easier to engage in the next two activities.
2. Listen to the discussants, and question them about their meaning, to confirm or modify your understanding of the speakers' points and so that the intended meaning becomes apparent to all.
3. Ask the discussants to defend their claims by developing arguments based on textual evidence that is fully interpreted.

OPENING THE DISCUSSION

The following practices are helpful for engaging the participants at the beginning of a group discussion:

1. All discussants and the leader should be seated in a circle.
2. Ask the discussants whether they have read or perused the entire text. Those who answer yes may participate in the discussion. Those who answer no should observe or retire to finish reviewing it.
3. Play the name game to be sure you and the other group members know the name of each participant. To begin, ask the group if the use of first names is

acceptable. If all agree, then ask the participant to your right to state his or her first name. The participant seated on his or her right repeats that name and adds his or her own name. The participants continue in like fashion, always repeating all the names in order and adding their own at the end of the list. As the last speaker, you repeat all names—backward as well as forward, if desired, adding your own name at the end. See chapter 4 for further discussion of the name game.

4. You may pose your prepared basic question or ask the discussants for their questions or comments. Or you may ask the discussants which approach they prefer. Regardless of the option chosen, the goal is the same: to reach a shared concern—a question that most, if not all, wish to address and make progress toward resolution.

Chapter 4 offers further ideas about opening the discussion.

LEADING STRATEGIES THAT HELP THE GROUP FORM AND PURSUE THE RESOLUTION OF THE SHARED QUESTION

Other than the first step (posing the basic question to launch the discussion), you can repeat the following practices when appropriate, to keep the discussion on the track of forming and addressing a shared point of doubt:

1. Pose the basic question to begin the discussion.
2. Ask the participants about the meaning of the text.
3. Suggest possible interpretations of the text.
4. Ask the participants for textual evidence, including its precise location (page numbers, paragraphs, line numbers, for example).
5. Repeat back what the participants have said to confirm or clarify their intended meaning.
6. Ask the participants directly about the meaning of their words.
7. Ask the discussants to address comments or questions raised by others.
8. Identify similarities and differences in comments and questions offered by the discussants.

See chapter 4 for further description of discussion-leading patterns.

ENDING THE DISCUSSION

As the discussion progresses, periodically summarize the progress that has been made. That is, pose the question that seems to be of concern, and if appropriate, relate it to other questions that have been explored. Also, restate the responses that have been given to the question thus far. In ending the discussion, it helps to repeat one last time the question or questions that have become the shared point of doubt. There is no need to force consensus about resolution, however. It is better to review possible resolutions that have been developed.

The discussion will often last forty-five minutes or more. Try to be sure that each student speaks at least three times, which means calling on the more reluctant participants. If you call on someone, it helps to say the name first, before posing the question, so that the respondent is alerted and has a chance to compose a response as he or she listens.

Notes

1. This handout refers to Sophie Haroutunian-Gordon's *Interpretive Discussion: Engaging Students in Text-Based Conversation* (Cambridge, MA: Harvard Education Press, 2014).

Text and Cluster of Questions for "Rats"

THE TEXT OF "Rats" is reprinted with permission from Houghton Mifflin Harcourt Publishing Company and Deutscher Taschenbuch Verlag (München, Germany). Konrad Lorenz, *On Aggression*, trans. Marjorie Kerr (Wien: Dr. G. Bortha, Schoeler Verlag, 1963). The excerpt appears in Nancy Carr, Joseph Coulson, and Mike Levin, eds., *The Nature of Life: Readings in Biology* (Chicago: Great Books Foundation, 2001), 177–179.[1]

TEXT OF "RATS"

1   Serious fights between members of
2   the same big family [of rats] occur in one situation only, which in many
3   respects is significant and interesting: such fights take place when a strange
4   rat is present and has aroused intraspecific, interfamily aggression. What
5   rats do when a member of a strange rat clan enters their territory or is put
6   in there by a human experimenter is one of the most horrible and repulsive
7   things which can be observed in animals. The strange rat may run around
8   for minutes on end without having any idea of the terrible fate awaiting it,
9   and the resident rats may continue for an equally long time with their ordi-
10 nary affairs till finally the stranger comes close enough to one of them for

11   it to get wind of the intruder. The information is transmitted like an electric
12   shock through the resident rat, and at once the whole colony is alarmed by
13   a process of mood transmission which is communicated in the brown rat
14   by expression movements but in the house rat by a sharp, shrill, satanic cry
15   which is taken up by all members of the tribe within earshot.

16   With their eyes bulging from their sockets, their hair standing on end,
17   the rats set out on the rat hunt. They are so angry that if two of them meet
18   they bite each other. "So they fight for three to five seconds," reports
19   Steiniger, "then with necks outstretched they sniff each other thoroughly
20   and afterward part peacefully. On the day of persecution of the strange rat
21   all the members of the clan are irritable and suspicious." Evidently the
22   members of a rat clan do not know each other personally, as jackdaws,
23   geese, and monkeys do, but they recognize each other by the clan smell, as
24   bees and insects do. A member of the clan can be branded as a hated
25   stranger, or vice versa, if its smell has been influenced one way or the other.
26   Eibl removed a rat from a colony and put it in another terrarium specially
27   prepared for the purpose. On its return to the clan enclosure a few days
28   later, it was treated as a stranger, but if the rat was put, together with some
29   soil, nest, etc., from this clan enclosure, into a clean, empty battery jar so
30   that it took with it a dowry of objects impregnated with a clan smell, it
31   would be recognized afterward, even after an absence of weeks.

32   Heartbreaking was the fate of a house rat which Eibl had treated in the
33   first way, and which in my presence he put back into the clan enclosure.
34   This animal had obviously not forgotten the smell of the clan, but it did not
35   know that its own smell was changed. So it felt perfectly safe and at home,
36   and the cruel bites of its former friends came as a complete surprise to it.
37   Even after several nasty wounds, it did not react with fear and desperate
38   flight attempts, as really strange rats do at the first meeting with an aggres-
39   sive member of the resident clan. To softhearted readers I give the assurance,
40   to biologists I admit hesitatingly, that in this case we did not await the bit-
41   ter end but put the experimental animal into a protective cage which we
42   then placed in the clan enclosure for repatriation.

43   Without such sentimental interference, the fate of the strange rat would
44   be sealed. The best thing that can happen to it is, as S. A. Barnett has
45   observed in individual cases, that it should die of shock. Otherwise it is
46   slowly torn to pieces by its fellows. Only rarely does one see an animal in
47   such desperation and panic, so conscious of the inevitability of a terrible
48   death, as a rat which is about to be slain by rats. It ceases to defend itself.
49   One cannot help comparing this behavior with what happens when a rat
50   faces a large predator that has driven it into a corner whence there is no
51   more escape than from the rats of a strange clan. In the face of death, it
52   meets the eating enemy with attack, the best method of defense, and springs
53   at it with the shrill war cry of its species.

54   What is the purpose of group hate between rat clans? What species-
55   preserving function has caused its evolution? The disturbing thought for the
56   human race is that this good old Darwinian train of thought can only be
57   applied where the causes which induce selection derive from the extraspe-
58   cific environment. Only then does selection bring about adaptation. But
59   wherever competition between members of a species effects sexual selection,
60   there is, as we already know, grave danger that members of a species may in
61   demented competition drive each other into the most stupid blind alley of
62   evolution … . [W]e have read of the wings of the Argus pheasant and the work-
63   ing pace of Western civilized man as examples of such efforts of evolution. It
64   is thus quite possible that the group hate between rat clans is really a diaboli-
65   cal invention which serves no purpose. On the other hand it is not impossible
66   that as-yet unknown external selection factors are still at work; we can, how-
67   ever, maintain with certainty that those indispensable species-preserving
68   functions of intraspecific aggression … are not served by clan fights. These
69   serve neither spatial distribution nor the selection of strong family defend-
70   ers—for among rats these are seldom the fathers of the descendants …

71   It can readily be seen that the constant warfare between large neigh-
72   boring families of rats must exert a huge selection pressure in the direction
73   of an ever increasing ability to fight, and that a rat clan which cannot keep
74   up in this respect must soon fall victim to extermination. Probably natural
75   selection has put a premium on the most highly populated families, since

76   the members of a clan evidently assist each other in fights against strangers,
77   and thus a smaller clan is at a disadvantage in fights against a larger one. On
78   the small North Sea island of Norderoog, Steiniger found that the ground
79   was divided between a small number of rat clans separated by a strip of
80   about fifty yards of no rat's land where fights were constantly taking place.
81   The front is relatively larger for a small clan than for a big one, and the
82   small one is therefore at a disadvantage.

CLUSTER OF QUESTIONS FOR "RATS"

Basic question: According to the text, why do rat clans hate one another?

Follow-up questions:

1. When Lorenz says, "Such fights take place when a strange rat is present and has aroused intraspecific, interfamily aggression" (3–4), does he mean that fights between rat clans ["intraspecific, interfamily aggression"] occur when an unknown rat is introduced to another rat group's territory, thereby drawing out a fighting response from the resident rats? If so, is the fighting response helpful to the rat species because over time, rats that hate "strangers" fight, survive, reproduce, and are better able to protect their territory and themselves?

2. When Lorenz says, "This good old Darwinian train of thought can only be applied where the causes which induce selection derive from the extraspecific environment" (56–58), does it mean that if hatred between rat clans is explained by saying it makes the rats more likely to survive, then the threat to their survival must come from outside their species? If so, do rat clans hate one another because by hating and fighting a strange rat that invades their territory, they practice a survival mechanism acquired through facing and defeating threats to their species over generations?

3. When Lorenz says, "Probably natural selection has put a premium on the most highly populated families, since the members of a clan evidently assist each other in fights against strangers" (74–76), does he mean that the largest clans of rats outlive other, smaller clans of rats because the larger clans of rats work together to fight strange rats and any other enemy species that invade their territory? If so, do rat clans hate one another because that hatred moves them to help other clan members destroy strangers

that invade their territory, and these aggressive, successful rats reproduce, thereby making the later generations of the clan ever larger?

4. When Lorenz says, "Wherever competition between members of a species effects sexual selection, there is, as we already know, grave danger that members of a species may in demented competition drive each other into the most stupid blind alley of evolution" (59–62), does he mean that the fighting between rats of the same species, but from different clans, which allows for only some rats to live long enough to reproduce, presents mortal danger to the entire species of rats? If so, is there no evolutionary explanation for why clans of rats fight or hate one another?

5. When Lorenz describes the situation in which a "colony is alarmed by a process of mood transmission which is communicated in the brown rat by expression movements but in the house rat by a sharp, shrill, satanic cry which is taken up by all members of the tribe within earshot" (12–15), does he mean that a clan of rats works together to fight off and kill a perceived intruding rat through a type of battle cry that rallies the rats in an effort to jointly fight this strange rat? If so, does the sound of the battle cry move the rats to attack the stranger and thereby set in motion the pattern of helping one another to that end, so that the strong, aggressive rats are the ones that survive and reproduce?

6. When Lorenz asks, "What species-preserving function has caused its [group hate between rat clans] evolution?" (54–55), does he ask if the rat clans hate one another because it helps them survive as a species? If so, does he suggest that hatred between rat clans exists because it helps them survive as a species?

7. When the text says that if the survival benefit is given, it must relate to "causes which induce selection … from the extraspecific environment. Only then does selection bring about adaptation" (57–58), does it mean that to give an evolutionary account of why rat clans hate one another, you must explain how a force outside the rat species could require the hatred between rat clans to ensure its survival? If so, does the text mean that to explain how hatred between rat clans could benefit the rat species, that force would need to be identified?

8. When the text says, "It can readily be seen that the constant warfare between large neighboring families of rats must exert a huge selection pressure in the direction of an ever increasing ability to fight, and that a rat

clan which cannot keep up in this respect must soon fall victim to extermination" (71–74), does it mean that because rat clans hate and fight one another, the characteristics that allow them to win in battle will survive and be passed down to new generations, so that those clans lacking these characteristics will die out? If so, do rat clans hate one another because the characteristics that allow them to win rat wars allow them to survive?

Notice that questions 1, 2, 3, 5, and 8 point to evidence for a possible resolution of the basic question, namely, Do rat clans hate one another because the hatred draws out their tendency to fight, and those who reproduce are those who fight and survive?

Notes

1. This handout refers to Sophie Haroutunian-Gordon's *Interpretive Discussion: Engaging Students in Text-Based Conversations* (Cambridge, MA: Harvard Education Press, 2014).

Text and Cluster of Questions for Toni Morrison's Nobel Laureate Lecture

THE TEXT OF Toni Morrison's Nobel Lecture is reprinted with permission from the Nobel Foundation. Toni Morrison, "Nobel Lecture" (Nobel Prize in Literature, Stockholm, Sweden, December 7, 1993).[1]

TEXT OF TONI MORRISON'S LECTURE

1   Thank you. My sincere thanks to the Swedish Academy. And thank you all for this very

2   warm welcome.

3   Fiction has never been entertainment for me. It has been the work I have done for most of

4   my adult life. I believe that one of the principal ways in which we acquire, hold, and

5   digest information is via narrative. So I hope you will understand when the remarks I

6   make begin with what I believe to be the first sentence of our childhood that we all

7   remember—the phrase "Once upon a time …"

8   "Once upon a time there was an old woman. Blind but wise." Or was it an old man? A

9   guru, perhaps. Or a griot soothing restless children. I have heard this story, or one exactly

10   like it, in the lore of several cultures.

11   "Once upon a time there was an old woman. Blind. Wise."

12   In the version I know the woman is the daughter of slaves, black, American, and lives

13   alone in a small house outside of town. Her reputation for wisdom is without peer and

14   without question. Among her people she is both the law and its transgression. The honor

15   she is paid and the awe in which she is held reach beyond her neighborhood to places far

16   away; to the city where the intelligence of rural prophets is the source of much

17   amusement.

18   One day the woman is visited by some young people who seem to be bent on disproving

19   her clairvoyance and showing her up for the fraud they believe she is. Their plan is

20   simple: they enter her house and ask the one question the answer to which rides solely on

21   her difference from them, a difference they regard as a profound disability: her blindness.

22   They stand before her, and one of them says, "Old woman, I hold in my hand a bird. Tell

23   me whether it is living or dead."

24   She does not answer, and the question is repeated. "Is the bird I am holding living or

25   dead?"

26   Still she doesn't answer. She is blind and cannot see her visitors, let alone what is in their

27   hands. She does not know their color, gender or homeland. She only knows their motive.

28   The old woman's silence is so long, the young people have trouble holding their laughter.

29   Finally she speaks and her voice is soft but stern. "I don't know," she says. "I don't know

30   whether the bird you are holding is dead or alive, but what I do know is that it is in your

31   hands. It is in your hands."

32   Her answer can be taken to mean: if it is dead, you have either found it that way or you

33   have killed it. If it is alive, you can still kill it. Whether it is to stay alive, it is your

34   decision. Whatever the case, it is your responsibility.

35   For parading their power and her helplessness, the young visitors are reprimanded, told

36   they are responsible not only for the act of mockery but also for the small bundle of life

37   sacrificed to achieve its aims. The blind woman shifts attention away from assertions of

38   power to the instrument through which that power is exercised.

39   Speculation on what (other than its own frail body) that bird-in-the-hand might signify

40   has always been attractive to me, but especially so now thinking, as I have been, about

41   the work I do that has brought me to this company. So I choose to read the bird as

42   language and the woman as a practiced writer. She is worried about how the language she

43   dreams in, given to her at birth, is handled, put into service, even withheld from her for

44   certain nefarious purposes. Being a writer she thinks of language partly as a system,

45   partly as a living thing over which one has control, but mostly as agency— as an act with

46   consequences. So the question the children put to her: "Is it living or dead?" is not unreal

47   because she thinks of language as susceptible to death, erasure; certainly imperiled and

48   salvageable only by an effort of the will. She believes that if the bird in the hands of her

49   visitors is dead the custodians are responsible for the corpse. For her a dead language is

50   not only one no longer spoken or written, it is unyielding language content to admire its

51   own paralysis. Like statist language, censored and censoring. Ruthless in its policing

52   duties, it has no desire or purpose other than maintaining the free range of its own

53   narcotic narcissism, its own exclusivity and dominance. However moribund, it is not

54   without effect for it actively thwarts the intellect, stalls conscience, suppresses human

55   potential. Unreceptive to interrogation, it cannot form or tolerate new ideas, shape other

56   thoughts, tell another story, fill baffling silences. Official language smitheryed to sanction

57   ignorance and preserve privilege is a suit of armor polished to shocking glitter, a husk

58 from which the knight departed long ago. Yet there it is: dumb, predatory, sentimental.

59 Exciting reverence in schoolchildren, providing shelter for despots, summoning false

60 memories of stability, harmony among the public.

61 She is convinced that when language dies, out of carelessness, disuse, indifference and

62 absence of esteem, or killed by fiat, not only she herself, but all users and makers are

63 accountable for its demise. In her country children have bitten their tongues off and use

64 bullets instead to iterate the voice of speechlessness, of disabled and disabling language,

65 of language adults have abandoned altogether as a device for grappling with meaning,

66 providing guidance, or expressing love. But she knows tongue-suicide is not only the

67 choice of children. It is common among the infantile heads of state and power merchants

68 whose evacuated language leaves them with no access to what is left of their human

69 instincts for they speak only to those who obey, or in order to force obedience.

70 The systematic looting of language can be recognized by the tendency of its users to

71 forgo its nuanced, complex, mid-wifery properties for menace and subjugation.

72 Oppressive language does more than represent violence; it is violence; does more than

73 represent the limits of knowledge; it limits knowledge. Whether it is obscuring state

74 language or the faux-language of mindless media; whether it is the proud but calcified

75 language of the academy or the commodity driven language of science; whether it is the

76 malign language of law-without-ethics, or language designed for the estrangement of

77 minorities, hiding its racist plunder in its literary cheek—it must be rejected, altered and

78 exposed. It is the language that drinks blood, laps vulnerabilities, tucks its fascist boots

79 under crinolines of respectability and patriotism as it moves relentlessly toward the

80 bottom line and the bottomed-out mind. Sexist language, racist language, theistic

81 language—all are typical of the policing languages of mastery, and cannot, do not permit

82 new knowledge or encourage the mutual exchange of ideas.

83 The old woman is keenly aware that no intellectual mercenary, nor insatiable dictator, no

84 paid-for politician or demagogue; no counterfeit journalist would be persuaded by her

85 thoughts. There is and will be rousing language to keep citizens armed and arming;

86 slaughtered and slaughtering in the malls, courthouses, post offices, playgrounds,

87 bedrooms and boulevards; stirring, memorializing language to mask the pity and waste of

88 needless death. There will be more diplomatic language to countenance rape, torture,

89 assassination. There is and will be more seductive, mutant language designed to throttle

90 women, to pack their throats like paté-producing geese with their own unsayable,

91 transgressive words; there will be more of the language of surveillance disguised as

92   research; of politics and history calculated to render the suffering of millions mute;

93   language glamorized to thrill the dissatisfied and bereft into assaulting their neighbors;

94   arrogant pseudo-empirical language crafted to lock creative people into cages of

95   inferiority and hopelessness.

96   Underneath the eloquence, the glamour, the scholarly associations, however stirring or

97   seductive, the heart of such language is languishing, or perhaps not beating at all—if the

98   bird is already dead.

99   She has thought about what could have been the intellectual history of any discipline if it

100   had not insisted upon, or been forced into, the waste of time and life that rationalizations

101   for and representations of dominance required—lethal discourses of exclusion blocking

102   access to cognition for both the excluder and the excluded.

103   The conventional wisdom of the Tower of Babel story is that the collapse was a

104   misfortune. That it was the distraction, or the weight of many languages that precipitated

105   the tower's failed architecture. That one monolithic language would have expedited the

106   building and heaven would have been reached. Whose heaven, she wonders? And what

107   kind? Perhaps the achievement of Paradise was premature, a little hasty if no one could

108   take the time to understand other languages, other views, other narratives period. Had

109 they, the heaven they imagined might have been found at their feet. Complicated,

110 demanding, yes, but a view of heaven as life; not heaven as post-life.

111 She would not want to leave her young visitors with the impression that language should

112 be forced to stay alive merely to be. The vitality of language lies in its ability to limn the

113 actual, imagined and possible lives of its speakers, readers, writers. Although its poise is

114 sometimes in displacing experience it is not a substitute for it. It arcs toward the place

115 where meaning may lie. When a President of the United States thought about the

116 graveyard his country had become, and said, "The world will little note nor long

117 remember what we say here. But it will never forget what they did here," his simple

118 words are exhilarating in their life-sustaining properties because they refused to

119 encapsulate the reality of 600,000 dead men in a cataclysmic race war. Refusing to

120 monumentalize, disdaining the "final word," the precise "summing up," acknowledging

121 their "poor power to add or detract," his words signal deference to the uncapturability of

122 the life it mourns. It is the deference that moves her, that recognition that language can

123 never live up to life once and for all. Nor should it. Language can never "pin down"

124 slavery, genocide, war. Nor should it yearn for the arrogance to be able to do so. Its force,

125 its felicity is in its reach toward the ineffable.

126 Be it grand or slender, burrowing, blasting, or refusing to sanctify; whether it laughs out

127 loud or is a cry without an alphabet, the choice word, the chosen silence, unmolested

128 language surges toward knowledge, not its destruction. But who does not know of

129 literature banned because it is interrogative; discredited because it is critical; erased

130 because alternate? And how many are outraged by the thought of a self-ravaged tongue?

131 Word-work is sublime, she thinks, because it is generative; it makes meaning that secures

132 our difference, our human difference—the way in which we are like no other life.

133 We die. That may be the meaning of life. But we do language. That may be the measure

134 of our lives.

135 "Once upon a time, …" visitors ask an old woman a question. Who are they, these

136 children? What did they make of that encounter? What did they hear in those final words:

137 "The bird is in your hands"? A sentence that gestures towards possibility or one that

138 drops a latch? Perhaps what the children heard was "It's not my problem. I am old,

139 female, black, blind. What wisdom I have now is in knowing I cannot help you. The

140 future of language is yours."

141 They stand there. Suppose nothing was in their hands? Suppose the visit was only a ruse,

142 a trick to get to be spoken to, taken seriously as they have not been before? A chance to

143   interrupt, to violate the adult world, its miasma of discourse about them, for them, but

144   never to them? Urgent questions are at stake, including the one they have asked: "Is the

145   bird we hold living or dead?" Perhaps the question meant: "Could someone tell us what is

146   life? What is death?" No trick at all; no silliness. A straightforward question worthy of

147   the attention of a wise one. An old one. And if the old and wise who have lived life and

148   faced death cannot describe either, who can?

149   But she does not; she keeps her secret; her good opinion of herself; her gnomic

150   pronouncements; her art without commitment. She keeps her distance, enforces it and

151   retreats into the singularity of isolation, in sophisticated, privileged space.

152   Nothing, no word follows her declaration of transfer. That silence is deep, deeper than the

153   meaning available in the words she has spoken. It shivers, this silence, and the children,

154   annoyed, fill it with language invented on the spot.

155   "Is there no speech," they ask her, "no words you can give us that helps us break through

156   your dossier of failures? Through the education you have just given us that is no

157   education at all because we are paying close attention to what you have done as well as to

158   what you have said? To the barrier you have erected between generosity and wisdom?

159   "We have no bird in our hands, living or dead. We have only you and our important

160   question. Is the nothing in our hands something you could not bear to contemplate, to

161   even guess? Don't you remember being young when language was magic without

162   meaning? When what you could say, could not mean? When the invisible was what

163   imagination strove to see? When questions and demands for answers burned so brightly

164   you trembled with fury at not knowing?

165   "Do we have to begin consciousness with a battle heroines and heroes like you have

166   already fought and lost leaving us with nothing in our hands except what you have

167   imagined is there? Your answer is artful, but its artfulness embarrasses us and ought to

168   embarrass you. Your answer is indecent in its self-congratulation. A made-for-television

169   script that makes no sense if there is nothing in our hands.

170   "Why didn't you reach out, touch us with your soft fingers, delay the sound bite, the

171   lesson, until you knew who we were? Did you so despise our trick, our modus operandi

172   you could not see that we were baffled about how to get your attention? We are young.

173   Unripe. We have heard all our short lives that we have to be responsible. What could that

174   possibly mean in the catastrophe this world has become; where, as a poet said, "nothing

175   needs to be exposed since it is already barefaced." Our inheritance is an affront. You

176   want us to have your old, blank eyes and see only cruelty and mediocrity. Do you think

177   we are stupid enough to perjure ourselves again and again with the fiction of nationhood?

178   How dare you talk to us of duty when we stand waist deep in the toxin of your past?

179   "You trivialize us and trivialize the bird that is not in our hands. Is there no context for

180   our lives? No song, no literature, no poem full of vitamins, no history connected to

181   experience that you can pass along to help us start strong? You are an adult. The old one,

182   the wise one. Stop thinking about saving your face. Think of our lives and tell us your

183   particularized world. Make up a story. Narrative is radical, creating us at the very

184   moment it is being created. We will not blame you if your reach exceeds your grasp; if

185   love so ignites your words they go down in flames and nothing is left but their scald. Or

186   if, with the reticence of a surgeon's hands, your words suture only the places where blood

187   might flow. We know you can never do it properly—once and for all. Passion is never

188   enough; neither is skill. But try. For our sake and yours forget your name in the street; tell

189   us what the world has been to you in the dark places and in the light. Don't tell us what to

190   believe, what to fear. Show us belief's wide skirt and the stitch that unravels fear's caul.

191   You, old woman, blessed with blindness, can speak the language that tells us what only

192   language can: how to see without pictures. Language alone protects us from the scariness

193   of things with no names. Language alone is meditation.

194 "Tell us what it is to be a woman so that we may know what it is to be a man. What

195 moves at the margin. What it is to have no home in this place. To be set adrift from the

196 one you knew. What it is to live at the edge of towns that cannot bear your company.

197 "Tell us about ships turned away from shorelines at Easter, placenta in a field. Tell us

198 about a wagonload of slaves, how they sang so softly their breath was indistinguishable

199 from the falling snow. How they knew from the hunch of the nearest shoulder that the

200 next stop would be their last. How, with hands prayered in their sex, they thought of heat,

201 then sun. Lifting their faces as though it was there for the taking. Turning as though there

202 for the taking. They stop at an inn. The driver and his mate go in with the lamp leaving

203 them humming in the dark. The horse's void steams into the snow beneath its hooves and

204 its hiss and melt are the envy of the freezing slaves.

205 "The inn door opens: a girl and a boy step away from its light. They climb into the wagon

206 bed. The boy will have a gun in three years, but now he carries a lamp and a jug of warm

207 cider. They pass it from mouth to mouth. The girl offers bread, pieces of meat and

208 something more: a glance into the eyes of the one she serves. One helping for each man,

209 two for each woman. And a look. They look back. The next stop will be their last. But not

210 this one. This one is warmed."

211 It's quiet again when the children finish speaking, until the woman breaks into the

212 silence.

213 "Finally," she says, "I trust you now. I trust you with the bird that is not in your hands

214 because you have truly caught it. Look. How lovely it is, this thing we have done—

215 together."

CLUSTER OF QUESTIONS FOR TONI MORRISON'S LECTURE

Basic question: Does the old woman come to trust the young people because she hears them trying to learn or because she hears them speaking the truth?

Follow-up questions:

1. When Toni Morrison says, "For parading their power and her helplessness, the young visitors are reprimanded, told they are responsible" (35), does she mean that at this point, the old woman does not trust the young people? If so, does she come to trust them because they rightly reprimand her (179–185) and, in so doing, speak the truth?

2. When Morrison says, "Sexist language, racist language, theistic language—all are typical of the policing languages of mastery, and cannot, do not permit new knowledge or encourage the mutual exchange of ideas" (80–82), does she mean that language that elevates some—for example, men over women, some races over others, a god or gods over humans—aims to enable some groups to control others, or to police them? If so, does the old woman not trust the young people at first because she thinks they are trying to control her? And does she come to trust them when she sees them trying to learn from her, as when they say, "Tell us what it is to be a woman so that we may know what it is to be a man. What moves at the margin. What it is to have no home no home in this place. To be set adrift from the one you knew" (195–197), which may mean, "Tell us about your experience of being a woman so that we will understand the nature of men and their relations to women; tell us what it means to be on the edge of

society rather than part of it; tell us what it feels like to live someplace and not feel at home; tell us what it means to be cast out of society," questions that they cannot but wish to answer?

3. When Morrison says in reference to the Tower of Babel, "Perhaps the achievement of Paradise was premature ... if no one could take the time to understand other languages, other views, other narratives period" (107–108), does she present the old woman's perspective? And is that perspective this: because people did not try to understand other people's languages, they did not try to understand each other's views, which was unwise? If so, does the old woman distrust the young people until they begin to use language to try to understand her views?

4. When Morrison says, "Language can never 'pin down' slavery, genocide, war. Nor should it yearn for the arrogance to be able to do so. Its force, its felicity is in its reach toward the ineffable" (123–125), does she mean that language should point to what cannot be said in words and, so, help us begin to understand those things? If so, does the old woman come to trust the young people when they ask to use language in that way, as when Morrison imagines them to be saying, "Could someone tell us what is life? What is death?" (145–146)?

5. When Morrison imagines the old woman thinking, "Word-work is sublime ... because it is generative; it makes meaning that secures our difference, our human difference—the way in which we are like no other life" (131–132), does she mean the old woman might believe that because human beings use words, they can give things meaning in speaking about them, which no other species can do? If so, does Morrison imagine that the old woman would want the young people to use language to express what is true about life?

6. When Morrison imagines, "Suppose the visit is only a ruse, a trick to get to be spoken to, taken seriously as they [the young people] have not been before? A chance to interrupt, to violate the adult world, its miasma of discourse about them, for them, but never to them ... No trick at all; no silliness" (141–145), does she mean that the young people may have come to the old woman seeking attention from an adult because adults do not talk to them but only about and on their behalf? If so, does Morrison suggest that the old woman may come to trust the young people because she sees that they want her attention to learn truth from her?

7. When Morrison imagines the young people saying, "Your answer is artful, but its artfulness embarrasses us and ought to embarrass you. Your answer is indecent in self-congratulation" (167–168), does she mean that the young people might be ridiculing the old woman for thinking up a response that is clever but does not address them in a meaningful way and thus is embarrassing? If so, might the old woman come to trust the young people because she sees they are right—that her response made no effort to know them?

8. When Morrison imagines the young people saying, "We are young. Unripe. We have heard all our short lives that we have to be responsible. What could that possibly mean in the catastrophe this world has become … Our inheritance is an affront. You want us to have your old, blank eyes and see only cruelty and mediocrity … How dare you talk to us of duty when we stand waist deep in the toxin of your past?" (172–178), does she imagine that the young people are challenging the old woman and are saying, "We are told to care for others and ourselves ("be responsible"), but the world you leave us is in shambles and offends us. Why should we tolerate unkind treatment and minimal treatment? And how can you ask us to care for others and ourselves when we live in a world that you have poisoned?"? If so, does the old woman come to trust the young people because she hears them speaking the truth?

9. When Morrison imagines the old woman as saying, "I trust you now. I trust you with the bird that is not in your hands because you have truly caught it. Look. How lovely it is, this thing we have done—together" (213–215), does she mean that the old woman comes to trust the young people because woman sees that they have learned the power of language—they have learned to use it? If so, when the old woman says that it is "lovely," does she mean that their response to her has made her trust them because they have used language to seek understanding from her? Or have they used it to speak the truth about her? Or to speak about the situation in the world?

Notes

1. This handout refers to Sophie Haroutunian-Gordon's *Interpretive Discussion: Engaging Students in Text-Based Conversations* (Cambridge, MA: Harvard Education Press, 2014).

The Nature
of Questions

QUESTIONS ABOUT THE MEANING of a text may be sorted into three categories: factual, evaluative, and interpretive. I borrow these designations and definitions from *Shared Inquiry Handbook: A Basic Guide for Discussion Leaders and Participants.*[1] A factual question is resolved by pointing to a place in the text that resolves the question definitively. An evaluative question is addressed by using criteria from outside the text to judge its truth, correctness, worth, or character. The interpretive question calls for further study of the text, as you cannot resolve the question definitively by pointing to only one place in the text. Thus, the interpretive question asks you to draw an inference about the meaning of the text in light of the evidence therein.[2]

In preparing to lead or participate in an interpretive discussion, you should write questions about the meaning of the text to be discussed while perusing it. *Be sure to number each question as you write, for ease of reference later.* Then sort the questions into the three categories—factual, evaluative, and interpretive. Usually, the sorting process is straightforward. However, sometimes it is not clear whether the question is factual, evaluative, or interpretive. To discover the category to which it belongs, start to answer the question. If you find yourself addressing it by pointing to a particular passage or place in the text, and you believe that the evidence there resolves the question definitively, then you have a factual question. If you find that you are addressing the question not by studying the text for evidence but by drawing on criteria from outside the text , then you have an evaluative question. If you find yourself looking at two or more places in the text that seem to address the issue, yet the evidence does not provide a definitive resolution, chances are that you have an interpretive question.

Here are some examples of questions that I wrote when perusing *Alice in Wonderland*, by Lewis Carroll:

- Does the Doormouse appear in the story each time Alice joins the Mad Hatter for tea? (factual question—can be answered definitively by looking at places where Alice and the Mad Hatter have tea)
- Is the Queen of Hearts ridiculous? (evaluative question—the answer depends on the reader's criteria for designating someone "ridiculous")
- According to the text, is the Queen of Hearts ridiculous? (may be an interpretive question, if the text offers criteria and the judgment is made with reference to these)
- Why does the Doormouse sleep so much? (probably insufficient textual evidence to address the question, in which case, the question is set aside as undiscussable)
- Does *Alice in Wonderland* present a child's view of the adult world or anyone's view of a mad world? (interpretive question—can be addressed with evidence from multiple places in the text, but not definitively)
- According to the text, do any of the characters in Wonderland like Alice? (worded as an interpretive question, as it asks that the judgment be made on the basis of criteria that the text presents)

Once you have written questions and categorized them as factual, evaluative, or interpretive, you are ready to begin scrutinizing the interpretive questions. If you are preparing to lead the discussion, these questions will be your starting point for the development of your cluster of questions. If you are preparing to participate in an interpretive discussion, you will identify the interpretive questions from your list (I ask participants to select two) and clarify them. While the factual and evaluative questions might well be asked in an interpretive discussion, they are set aside while you prepare yourself to lead or participate in the discussion, since further refinement of these questions does not help you cultivate a question about the meaning of the text that you care to resolve.

Notes

1. Donald H. Whitfield and Daniel Born, eds., *Shared Inquiry Handbook: A Basic Guide for Discussion Leaders and Participants* (Chicago: Great Books Foundation, 2007).
2. This handout refers to Sophie Haroutunian-Gordon's *Interpretive Discussion: Engaging Students in Text-Based Conversations* (Cambridge, MA: Harvard Education Press, 2014).

Overview: Preparing to Participate in Interpretive Discussion

DEVELOPING QUESTIONS YOU WISH TO RESOLVE ABOUT THE MEANING OF THE TEXT

The goal of the interpretive discussion is to come to a shared point of doubt about the meaning of the text under consideration. To achieve that goal, each discussant needs to have read the text prior to the discussion and prepared two interpretive questions about its meaning. I recommend that you, as a participant, proceed as described below:[1]

1. Read and study the text, and write questions about its meaning *as you read*. Be sure to number the questions, noting the page numbers or other locations to which the questions refer. Review the text a second time, adding questions to your list if more occur to you.

2. Read your questions. If some are factual or evaluative, set these aside. Looking at your interpretive questions, decide if some relate to others and if there are one or two issues about the meaning of the text that you might care to resolve.

Perhaps your deepest point of doubt—the question you wish most to resolve—has not been posed directly or clearly yet. Your goal, in reviewing your questions, is to identify that question.

Once you have identified the question, the next challenge is to clarify it—to make sure that it asks exactly what you want to know. To meet that challenge, I suggest that you do the following:

1. Look for places in the text that seem to suggest ideas about the answer to your point of doubt.
2. Quote the words, or describe the location of the text that suggests an idea about the answer to your question.
3. Indicate the exact location of the quoted words.
4. Interpret the quoted words fully. That is, say in your own words, no more and no less, than what the quoted words seem to mean. *Here you have the most crucial step:* even if you think the meaning of the quoted words is unambiguous, write out what you think the words say, no more and no less. Often, you will discover ambiguities that were not apparent when you read the words.
5. Passages often contain technical terms, that is, terms that could have more than one meaning, and the intended meaning is not clear. Words like "learning," "environment," "collaboration," "facilitator," "hands-on learning," and "hands-on experience" are but a few of examples of technical terms encountered regularly in the field of education. When you interpret quoted words that include technical terms, replace them with what the text seems to mean by them.
6. Use the quoted words, now that you have interpreted them, to suggest an idea about the resolution of your question.

The most efficient form of a sentence that expresses your interpretive question reads like this:

> When the text says, _____ [quote the words you wish to interpret] on page _____, does it mean _____ [say no more and no less than what the quoted words say]? If so, _____ [state the resolution of your question that is suggested by the quoted words, as interpreted].

See appendixes C and D for examples of good interpretive questions and statements.

STANDARDS OF CLARITY FOR YOUR QUESTIONS

The refined interpretive question should meet the following standards of clarity. These criteria are a subset of those presented in "Evaluating the Cluster of Questions," in chapter 3. The question should meet the following standards:

- Clearly express your point of doubt—what you do not know and do you wish to resolve about the meaning of the text (criterion 2).
- Connect your question to a passage that suggests an idea about the answer, with the location indicated precisely (criterion 4).
- Quote and fully interpret words that suggest some answer to your question (criterion 4).
- Interpret the quoted words with words that contain no technical terms or vague phrases (criterion 3).
- Suggest an idea about the resolution of your question—a resolution for which the quoted words offer evidence (criterion 6).

Writing an interpretive question that meets the above criteria is not easy. But in working to meet the goal, you help yourself find more and more meaning in the text.

By entering the discussion with two interpretive questions as described above, you come with queries that motivate participation and with the insight you gained through your preparation. Bring your two typed or written interpretive questions, together with the text, to the interpretive discussion.

Best of luck! Enjoy the experience.

Notes

1. This handout refers to Sophie Haroutunian-Gordon's *Interpretive Discussion: Engaging Students in Text-Based Conversations* (Cambridge, MA: Harvard Education Press, 2014).

Notes

Introduction

1. Jean Anyon, "Social Class and the Hidden Curriculum of Work," *Journal of Education* 162 (1980): 67–92.

2. Plato, *The Republic of Plato*, 2nd ed., ed. and trans. Allan Bloom (New York: Basic Books, 1991); Jean-Jacques Rousseau, *Emile, or On Education*, ed. and trans. Allan Bloom (New York: Basic Books, 1979); John Dewey, *Democracy and Education* (New York: Macmillan, 1916).

3. Hans-Georg Gadamer, *Truth and Method*, ed. Garrett Barden and John Cumming (New York: Crossroad, 1985); Hans Robert Jauss, *Question and Answer: Forms of Dialogic Understanding* (Minneapolis: University of Minnesota Press, 1989); Mikhail Mikhailovitch Bakhtin, "Discourse in the Novel," in *The Dialogic Imagination*, trans. and ed. Caryl Emerson and Michael Holquist (Austin: University of Texas Press, 1981); Paul Grice, *Studies in the Way of Words* (Cambridge, MA: Harvard University Press, 1989); Wolfgang Iser, *The Act of Reading: A Theory of Aesthetic Response* (Baltimore: Johns Hopkins University Press, 1980); Denis Donoghue, *The Practice of Reading* (New Haven: Yale University Press, 1998); Louise M. Rosenblatt, *Literature as Exploration* (New York: Modern Language Association, 1995); Roy D. Pea, "The Social and Technological Dimensions of Scaffolding and Related Theoretical Concepts for Learning, Education, and Human Activity," *Journal of the Learning Sciences* 13, no. 3 (2004): 423–451; Daniel C. Edelson and Brian J. Reiser, "Making Authentic Practices Accessible to Learners: Design Challenges and Strategies," in *Cambridge Handbook of the Learning Sciences*, ed. R. Keith Sawyer (New York: Cambridge University Press, 2006), 335–354; Lauren B. Resnick, *Education and Learning to Think* (Washington, DC: National Academy Press, 1987); Alan H. Schoenfeld, ed., *Mathematical Thinking and Problem Solving* (Hillsdale, NJ: Lawrence Erlbaum Associates, 1994); Jean Lave, "Situated Learning in Communities of Practice," in *Perspectives on Socially Shared Cognition*, ed. Lauren B. Resnick, John M. Levine, and Stephanie D.

Teaseley (Washington, DC: American Psychological Association, 1991); Jean Lave and Etienne Wenger, *Situated Learning: Legitimate Peripheral Participation* (New York: Cambridge University Press, 1991).

4. Sophie Haroutunian-Gordon, *Learning to Teach Through Discussion: The Art of Turning the Soul* (New Haven: Yale University Press, 2009), 1–18.

5. P. Karen Wilkinson Murphy et al., "Examining the Effects of Classroom Discussion on Students' Comprehension of Text: A Meta-analysis," *Journal of Educational Psychology* 101, no. 3 (2009): 740–764, compares approaches to classroom discussions (such as Collaborative Reasoning, Paideia Seminar, Philosophy for Children, Instructional Conversations, Junior Great Books Shared Inquiry, Questioning the Author, Book Club, Grand Conversations, and Literature Circles) and shows that they differ with respect to their treatment of the text. For example, while Junior Great Books stresses text interpretation, Questioning the Author strives to help discussants grasp what the author intended. Philosophy for Children emphasizes student responses to the moral dilemmas presented in the texts.

6. For example, Anyon, "Social Class and the Hidden Curriculum of Work," observes that interpretive-discussion-like activities were not found in classrooms where students were identified as low achievers.

7. Great Books Foundation and Junior Great Books discussions pursue shared inquiry with students. Donald H. Whitfield and Daniel Born, eds., *Shared Inquiry Handbook™: A Basic Guide for Discussion Leaders and Participants* (Chicago: Great Books Foundation, 2007).

8. Curt Dudley-Marling and Sarah Michaels, eds., *High-Expectation Curricula: Helping All Students Succeed with Powerful Learning* (New York: Teachers College Press, 2012).

9. For example, Richard Allington maintains that making "text to self" connections helps discussants express their responses to texts, in light of their personal experiences and feelings. Richard L. Allington, *What Really Matters for Struggling Readers: Designing Research-Based Programs* (New York: Addison Wesley Longman, 2001).

10. Sophie Haroutunian-Gordon, "Listening to a Challenging Perspective: The Role of Interruption," *Teachers College Record* 112, no. 1 (2010) 2793–2814 (Special Issue on Listening, ed. Sophie Haroutunian-Gordon and Leonard Waks).

11. Haroutunian-Gordon, *Learning to Teach Through Discussion*, 144–151.

12. Ibid., especially ch. 6.

13. Elizabeth Meadows, "Learning to Listen to Differences: Democracy, Dewey, and Interpretive Discussion," *Journal of Curriculum Studies*, published online 2013 (DOI: 10.1080/00220272.2013.764021).

14. Richard Shweder, "What About Female Genital Mutilation?" in *Engaging in Cultural Differences: The Multicultural Challenge in Liberal Democracies*, ed. Richard Shweder et al. (New York: Russell Sage, 2002), 216–251.

15. Danielle S. Allen, *Talking to Strangers* (Chicago: University of Chicago Press, 2004).

16. Robin Milner-Gulland and Peter Levi, trans., *Selected Poems by Yevtushenko* (Baltimore: Penguin Books, 1962), 67–68.

17. Throughout the book, the names of the schools, the teachers in the schools, and the discussion participants are pseudonyms.

18. Dudley-Marling and Michaels, "Shared Inquiry: Making Students Smart," in *High-Expectations Curricula: Helping All Students Succeed with Powerful Learning*, ed. Curt Dudley-Marling and Sarah Michaels (New York: Teachers College Press, 2012), argue, from data, that "low achieving" students benefit from opportunities to engage in Shared Inquiry, an activity similar to interpretive discussion. They would agree with Jason's claim that special-education students can profitably engage in the latter.

Chapter 1

1. Jean Lave and Etienne Wenger, *Situated Learning: Legitimate Peripheral Participation* (New York: Cambridge University Press, 1991), present a framework for analyzing the kind of learning that takes place as people participate in interpretive discussion. As discussants become engaged in the practices of discussion, they gradually begin to initiate the productive practices. The discussants learn through what Lave and Wenger call "legitimate peripheral participation."

2. Reviewing the text but then posing questions prepared by another, or even by yourself previously, is often inadequate preparation. By so doing, you cannot become familiar with the text, or refresh your familiarity with it—something that cluster preparation and revision provides. Moreover, the borrowed question is often not of pressing concern to you. As a consequence, you might not come to the discussion as a seeker of understanding about the meaning of the text.

3. Students' names can be learned quickly by playing the name game, which I describe in chapter 4.

4. John Dewey, *The Later Works, 1925–1953*, vol. 8, *1933 Essays and How We Think*, rev. ed., ed. Jo Ann Boydston (Carbondale: Southern Illinois University Press, 1989), 196–200.

5. Donald Schön, *Educating the Reflective Practitioner* (San Francisco: Jossey-Bass Publishers, 1988).

6. Ibid., 5.

7. A discussion-leading pattern tells the listener the kind of response that is desired, although not the content of the response. A corresponding listening pattern is followed when the listener provides the kind of response that has been called for. As will be seen, people who participate in interpretive discussion begin to initiate both the discussion-leading and listening patterns in which they have been engaged.

Chapter 2

1. Sophie Haroutunian-Gordon, *Learning to Teach Through Discussion: The Art of Turning the Soul* (New Haven: Yale University Press, 2009). The book describes a case study in which two groups of fourth-grade students engage in a series of interpretive discussions.
2. Ibid., 166.
3. The point here is that until ambiguity has been identified, discussion about the meaning of the text cannot properly begin.
4. Sometimes, ambiguity can be found by relating texts to one another. For example, by juxtaposing drafts of the Declaration of Independence, you see possibilities for meaning that are not apparent when you view the various versions in isolation from one another. See the conclusion, in which Megan and Adam, teachers who conduct interpretive discussions, propose the practice of relating different texts to one another.
5. William E. Empson, *Seven Types of Ambiguity* (New York: New Directions, 1947), 1.
6. Michael Alexander Kirkwood Halliday, *Language as a Social Semiotic: A Social Interpretation of Language and Meaning* (Baltimore: University Park Press, 1978).
7. Michael Alexander Kirkwood Halliday and Ruqaiya Hasan, *Cohesion in English* (London: Longman, 1976), 5–6. See also Halliday, *Language as a Social Semiotic*, ch. 7.
8. Halliday, *Language as a Social Semiotic*, 128–130.
9. Ibid., 136.
10. Ibid., 141.
11. Haroutunian-Gordon, *Learning to Teach Through Discussion*, 7; William Iser, *The Act of Reading: A Theory of Aesthetic Response* (Baltimore: Johns Hopkins University Press, 1980).
12. Konrad Lorenz, "Rats," in *The Nature of Life: Readings in Biology*, ed. Nancy Carr, Joseph Coulson, and Mike Levin (Chicago: The Great Books Foundation, 2001), 177–179.
13. Master of Science in Education Program, School of Education and Social Policy, Northwestern University.
14. According to Halliday, the "environment" includes the genre of the text (here, a scientific analysis), its field (the setting in which the action of the text is located), its tenor (the relations and emotions between the participants), and the mode or kind of language communication adopted. Peter S. Doughty, John J. Pierce, and Geoffrey M. Thornton, *Exploring Language*, Explorations in Language Study series (London: Edward Arnold, 1972), quoted in Halliday, *Language as a Social Semiotic*, 33.
15. Toni Morrison, "Nobel Lecture" (Nobel Prize in Literature, Stockholm, Sweden, December 7, 1993).
16. The identification of an ambiguity in a text is a function of both the object and the leader perusing it, not the object in and of itself, apart from the leader. However, some

objects are more ambiguous than others, meaning that more questions about their meaning may be raised and their resolution pursued through study of the text.

Chapter 3

1. Consider the case in which discussants overlook facts in the text that are relevant to the point of doubt under consideration. In such a case, the leader might ask a factual question—a question that directs the discussants to evidence that resolves a question definitively and helps the group move toward resolution of a shared concern.

2. Here and in the chapters that follow, I borrow the designations and definitions of "fact" (or "factual"), "evaluative," and "interpretive" questions from Donald H. Whit- field and Daniel Born, eds., *Shared Inquiry Handbook: A Basic Guide for Discussion Leaders and Participants* (Chicago: Great Books Foundation, 2007). Discussants can resolve a fact question without debate by pointing to one place in the text. They can resolve an evaluative question by using criteria from outside the text to judge the text's correctness, worth, or character. The interpretive question calls for further study of the text; discussants cannot resolve the question definitively by pointing to one place in the text. Thus, the interpretive question asks the discussants to draw an inference about the meaning of the text in light of the evidence therein.

3. When you first begin writing questions, especially if you are unfamiliar with the text, many of the questions come out in "open" form, as you have no ideas to suggest about resolution. As you continue to peruse the text and write more questions, ideas about the answers begin to arise. Those ideas are often expressed in the form of questions about the meaning of passages that suggest the ideas.

4. The leader may have given up the issue too quickly, as sometimes happens.

5. I say "candidate for the deepest point of doubt" because the question selected may be modified as follow-up questions are written. Sometimes, in that process, it becomes clear that another question is of greater concern than the one designated at first.

6. The number eight is a rule of thumb—a goal. If you can write eight follow-up ques- tions, the ambiguity—indeed, the discussability—of the text has been demonstrated. In principle, it should take at least forty-five minutes to explore those eight passages. Still, seven follow-up questions might be sufficient to show that the text is ambiguous enough to sustain a forty-five-minute discussion about its meaning.

7. Sophie Haroutunian-Gordon, *Learning to Teach Through Discussion: The Art of Turning the Soul* (New Haven: Yale University Press, 2009), 94–95.

8. To test whether the basic question states the deepest point of doubt (criterion 5), read through the eight follow-up questions. Does resolving each one in at least one way sug- gest an idea about the resolution of the basic question? Or, do the possible resolutions

that occur suggest that the author of the cluster is in doubt about something other than the issue posed by the basic question?

9. The criteria were applied to the original set of follow-up questions before the discussion at the Aurora School took place. The cluster, as it existed at that time, was presented in chapter 1. When reviewing the original follow-up questions in writing the present chapter, I found that the criteria inspired further clarifications. Such is often the case. Hence, the revisions that follow differ from those found in the cluster given in chapter 1.

10. By expressing the basic question in issue form, the questioner expresses his or her best guess about the answer—*X* or *Y*. The discussants can begin the conversation by evaluating the suggestions offered. The reader may object that by writing the question in this way, the leader is telling the discussants what to think about the answer to the question. However, the discussants quickly realize that the presence of a suggestion in the basic question does not make it the correct answer. Even if they accept a suggested resolution, they must explain why it is correct, given the textual evidence.

Chapter 4

1. Sophie Haroutunian-Gordon, *Learning to Teach Through Discussion: The Art of Turning the Soul* (New Haven: Yale University Press, 2009). See ibid., ch. 6, for a detailed description of the patterns and an analysis of empirical data showing that some become more prevalent as leaders gain discussion leading experience.

2. Interpretive discussion groups in elementary and middle school grades might range in size from six to ten students, depending on age, discussion experience, and subject matter. See the case study reported in ibid., where the two groups of fourth-grade students were ten each. In chapter 5 of the present book, we consider one option for managing a larger class.

3. Since equal air time requires the participants to speak at least three times, it allows all to develop the speaking and listening skills required for successful discussion participation. As groups work together, the speaking time among participants tends to equalize. Ibid., 159.

4. I have never encountered a group that questioned the use of first names, but it could happen. In that case, it would be necessary to decide, by majority rule, whether surnames, surnames with titles, or first names should be invoked. See chapter 5, in the discussion of "Rats," where the classroom teacher participated as a coleader and the naming practice was not quite as described here.

5. It is important to avoid all distraction when playing the name game. Distractions can interfere with the learning. I have sometimes learned more than sixty names at once

in the manner described. The trick is to focus attention on each speaker and on the recitation of names as each speaker performs it.

6. While the leader may forget a name in the course of the discussion, the participants are generally forgiving, perhaps because they have seen that the leader wants to know the names.

7. The three parts of the argument given here are consistent with Stephen Toulmin's observation that the primary function of an argument is to provide justification for a claim. Here, what Toulmin calls the "claim" is the proffered interpretation; what he calls the "data" is the evidence from the text that is said to support the interpretation (steps 1 and 2 in the sidebar "Using Text to Support a Claim"). What he calls the "warrant" is the rule according to which we reason from the textual evidence to the claim about the interpretation (step 3 in the sidebar). We can accept the claim (conclusion) because it is justified by data. Stephen Edelston Toulmin, *The Uses of Argument* (London: Cambridge University Press, 1969), ch. 3.

8. As Halliday might argue, perhaps Michael is focused on the "mode" of the text, namely, its genre, and is thinking about the fact that it is a poem in his search for meaning.

9. Creating a queue of speakers may seem to have disadvantages. Might a speaker further down in the queue have forgotten what he or she wished to say in the intervening time? Might the contribution given later be irrelevant? In fact, the practice teaches discussants to write down their ideas and, if necessary, return the conversation to a topic from which it has veered. It also allows those wishing to speak to put their hands down and listen to others as they await their turns.

10. Halliday would say that identifying theme involves recognizing a rule that belongs to the category that he called "textual" rules. A theme is the practice of repeating an idea in various ways in a text.

Chapter 5

1. The fishbowl approach enables the teacher to create small groups within a large class. Those in the group of ten to fifteen discussants have the opportunity to develop both listening and speaking skills: they may respond to and initiate the discussion-leading patterns and so may answer and pose questions, offer and seek clarification of meaning, offer and seek claims about the meaning of the text, seek and identify textual evidence to support the claims, interpret or ask others to interpret the evidence, take positions on issues raised by others, and specify similarities and differences between positions that they hear. The observers develop listening skills, as they attend to what is said by others. But they do not follow the listening patterns practiced by those whom they observe, as the observers are not allowed to speak. As we will see, however, they

attend to what is said and thus prepare themselves to further the conversation when it is their turn to participate in the discussion.

2. Or as Halliday might say, reading sentences that precede or follow a perplexing state-ment can help you follow the semantic rules (e.g., ideational, interpersonal, textual). See chapter 2, and Michael Alexander Kirkwood Halliday, *Language as a Social Semi-otic: A Social Interpretation of Language and Meaning* (Baltimore: University Park Press, 1978), 128–130.

3. Over the course of ten discussions followed in Sophie Haroutunian-Gordon, *Learning to Teach Through Discussion: The Art of Turning the Soul* (New Haven: Yale University Press, 2009), 119–131, the participants became better at using the text to formulate arguments. The number of evaluative comments decreased, while the number of spon-taneous references to the text (i.e., references to the text that were not prompted by the leader) increased. The leaders also exhibited productive discussion-leading patterns, particularly those related to clarifying the meaning of statements made by discussants, with greater frequency in the later discussions.

Chapter 6

1. To learn the names quickly, I played the name game with the group, as described in chapter 4.

2. Donald H. Whitfield and Daniel Born, eds., *Shared Inquiry Handbook: A Basic Guide for Discussion Leaders and Participants* (Chicago: Great Books Foundation, 2007), defines an "evaluative" discussion as one in which participants bring to bear their own criteria in judging a text—criteria that arise from their personal experiences rather than those provided by the text itself. When discussants depart from answering factual questions that can be resolved by pointing to a passage that resolves them definitively, or address-ing interpretive questions by studying textual evidence, they are said to be evaluating the text. Because some of the discussants at the Canterbury School open the conversa-tion by sharing what they mean by "taking responsibility," they are initially engaged in an evaluative rather than an interpretive discussion.

3. Sophie Haroutunian-Gordon, "Learning to Interpret Texts: Engaging Students in Rigorous Discussion," in *High-Expectation Curricula: Helping All Students Succeed with Powerful Learning*, ed. Curt Dudley-Marling and Sarah Michaels (New York: Teach-ers College Press, 2012), 95, identifies "Marisa" as the speaker. However, further study of the tape revealed that the question had been posed by Sonya.

4. Here, Eban makes an evaluative comment rather than an interpretive one, as the cri-teria for what it means to "take responsibility" come from his own experience rather than the text.

5. In Haroutunian-Gordon, "Learning to Interpret Texts," I offer analyze additional excerpts from the discussion in which we see Sonya, Larry, Dave and others learning to do line-by-line analysis of the text.

Chapter 7

1. Donald H. Whitfield and Daniel Born, eds., *Shared Inquiry Handbook: A Basic Guide for Discussion Leaders and Participants* (Chicago: The Great Books Foundation, 2007).
2. See chapter 2, and Michael Alexander Kirkwood Halliday, *Language as a Social Semiotic: A Social Interpretation of Language and Meaning* (Baltimore: University Park Press, 1978), 128–130.
3. The comments made by Durant and Jack are what the Great Books Foundation calls evaluative comments. That is, they are based on criteria that come from the reader's personal experience, not the evidence in the text.
4. The speakers focus on what they themselves think it means to "take responsibility," not what the old woman in the story might mean by the phrase.
5. Recall the three productive habits of mind exercised by interpretive discussion leaders: listen to grasp the speaker's intended meaning, listen to identify the speaker's question and ideas about resolution, and listen to determine the strength of the speaker's argument for resolving the question. Here, I argue that the leader exercises two and possibly all three habits of mind.
6. Sophie Haroutunian-Gordon, *Learning to Teach Through Discussion: The Art of Turning the Soul* (New Haven: Yale University Press, 2009), 12 and 16. See the formation of what Hans-Georg Gadamer, *Truth and Method*, ed. Garrett Barden and John Cumming (New York: Crossroad, 1985), calls the "object" of the conversation. In the discussion, an "object," or answer to the shared point of doubt that concerned the group, seems to arise out of the conversation—one that draws applause.

Conclusion

1. In the fall of 2011, I surveyed alumni of the Master of Science in Education Program, Northwestern University. All respondents had completed a philosophy of education course in which they not only participated in discussions but also prepared for, and coled, the discussions. In developing a master's thesis, each respondent had created a cluster of questions for, and led an interpretive discussion about, an article that was related to the question under investigation. Seventy-five people responded to the survey. Of that number, thirty-two agreed to be interviewed. The comments and dialogue excerpts that follow were culled from those interviews.
2. As a reminder, the names of the teachers given here are pseudonyms.

3. I again use the word "evaluative," as does the Great Books Foundation, to mean dialogue that seeks not to interpret but instead to judge the correctness or truth of ideas.

4. You might say that the students prefer to address factual or evaluative questions rather than interpretive ones.

Acknowledgments

THERE ARE MANY to thank for assistance of various sorts—assistance that has made possible what is now the third in a series of works on interpretive discussion. While space limits my ability to mention all who have contributed, unfortunately, here is a start.

I thank the following individuals and publishers who have allowed me to reprint texts and portions of texts in the book. Without their cooperation, the book would not have been possible:

Professor Robin Milner-Gulland and Penguin-Books, Ltd., for permission to reprint the English translation of the poem *Schoolmaster*, by Yevgeny Yevtushenko.

The excerpt from *On Aggression*, by Konrad Lorenz, translated by Marjorie Kerr. Copyright © 1963 by Dr. G. Bortha, Schoeler Verlag, Wien. Translation © 1966 by Konrad Lorenz. Reprinted in the United States by permission of Houghton Mifflin Harcourt Publishing Company. All rights reserved. Reprinted outside the United States by permission of Deutscher Taschenbuch Verlag, München, Germany, © 1983.

The excerpt from *On Aggression*, by Konrad Lorenz, appears in *The Nature of Life: Readings in Biology*. Copyright © 2001 by The Great Books Foundation, Chicago.

The Nobel Foundation for permission to reprint the Nobel Lecture delivered by Toni Morrison on December 7, 1993, © The Nobel Foundation, 1993.

Several individuals contributed to the creation of the book in a variety of ways. To begin with, I am grateful to Zhen Ye (Fiona), a master's student from China, who read my work and asked to spend a year with me as a research assistant to learn about interpretive discussion. From March 2011 to March 2012, she gave of her time freely to help me study transcripts and to deepen my insight as we listened to tapes of both leaders and participants in interpretive discussions. She also assisted with the preparation and deployment of a survey and follow-up interviews that are discussed in the conclusion. I am sincerely grateful to Fiona for her patience, dedication, and assistance.

I have also been most ably assisted by staff of the Master of Science in Education Program, Northwestern University. Sugandhi Chugani, Philip Kojo Clarke, Margaret Cramer, Annie Heller, Leslie Lepeska, and Bradley Wadle worked to secure permissions from publishers to reprint texts and excerpts from texts that appear in the book. All of them also assisted me in retrieving references from libraries and elsewhere. Joel Pollack, an alumnus of the program, assisted me in understanding relations between interpretive discussion and the Common Core State Standards. Finally, Bradley Wadle has worked untiringly and with great skill and dedication to help prepare the manuscript. I am deeply indebted to him and to all the others for their efforts.

My colleagues at Northwestern University, including Matt Easterbrook, Carol Lee, Steven McGee, Brian Reiser, Miriam Sherin, and Uri Wilensky, have challenged my thinking on many issues related to interpretive discussion.

To my many students in the Master of Science in Education Program over the period of twenty-two years, I owe a profound debt of gratitude—one that I can never adequately acknowledge. They have taught me much of what I have learned about all the phases of interpretive discussion: the importance and the power of careful preparation; the joy of individuals working together to achieve new understanding of the text; the nature of effective discussion-leading patterns; the importance of listening and how to make it effective. The insights I have gleaned while working with our teacher candidates—indeed, some of them over many years, as they return to Northwestern to serve as teaching assistants—have guided me through analysis and practice time and again over these pages.

In particular, I acknowledge the alumni who have played a dramatic part in the book. "Ms. Bright" and "Ms. Prentice" graciously invited me into their classrooms and thus made possible the discussions of Yevtushenko's *Schoolmaster* and Konrad Lorenz's "Rats." It was a joy to work with both of them—and with their students.

Furthermore, I am truly grateful to the alumni who speak in the conclusion of the book. All of them gave generously of their time in both responding to a survey about their experiences with interpretive discussion and providing me with additional comments that helped clarify and amplify their views. While I identify them only with pseudonyms, the reader should know that they are experienced, dedicated teachers in whose classrooms interpretive discussion is alive and well. May their words inspire readers as these professionals have inspired me, their teacher.

My work with teacher candidates, particularly "Marsha" and "Paula," whom I studied as they learned to lead discussions (see my *Learning to Teaching Through Conversation: The Art of Turning the Soul*, 2009), sensitized me to the critical role of listening in conversations: you cannot ask good questions of participants if you cannot understand what they intend to say. For more than ten years now, I have explored the topic of listening with colleagues from around the United States and abroad. In particular, I thank Nick Burbules, Kerrie Embrey, Andrea English, Jim Garrison, Allison Hintz, Winifred Hunsburger, Orit Kent, Megan Laverty, Elizabeth Meadows, Bruce Novak, Suzanne Rice, A. G. Rud, Kathy Schultz, Deborah Seltzer-Kelly, Kersti Tyson, Leonard Waks, and Stanton Wortham, all of whom have enriched my appreciation of listening so much.

I am indebted to my colleagues René Arcilla, Curt Dudley-Marling, Sharon Feiman-Nemser, Walter Feinberg, David Hansen, and Sarah Michaels, who, along with their students on a variety of occasions, have challenged my thinking about interpretive discussion in many fruitful ways over the years. My most sincere thanks to each of them.

I acknowledge with deep appreciation my editor from the Harvard Education Press, Caroline Chauncey. She has been committed to the project since first reading my *Learning to Teach Through Discussion: The Art of Turning the Soul*. Persuaded of the value and potential usefulness of interpretive discussion as pedagogical orientation, she recognized it as especially critical at a time when many states have adopted the Common Core State Standards, which call for rigorous thinking throughout the curriculum. Ms. Chauncey has worked with me for more than three years, reading drafts of chapters and offering insightful suggestions that helped these to become clear and accessible. I benefited again and again from her perceptiveness, skill, insight, patience, and encouragement.

Finally, two more people have stood by me steadfastly in my study of interpretive discussion. Penelope Peterson, Dean of the School of Education and Social Policy, Northwestern University, has given unflagging support over many years to the work, including the resources needed to make interpretive discussion the leitmotif of the Master of Science in Education Program. And my husband, Robert P. Gordon, has heard more about interpretive discussion than he ever imagined he might. But we are still married, still questioning, still listening, and still working to interpret the text that we have been creating with one another for nearly thirty years.

About the Author

Sophie Haroutunian-Gordon has served as professor and director of the Master of Science in Education Program (MSEd) at Northwestern University for twenty-two years; she retired as director in August 2013. At the start of her professional career, she taught sixth grade for five years, then earned a PhD at the University of Chicago, where she joined the faculty. In 1991, she went to Northwestern. An educational philosopher by training, she is a past president of the Philosophy of Education Society (2003). She conducts research on topics related to the philosophy of education, including interpretive discussion, that is, discussion about the meaning of texts. She has written three books on the topic, the first of which, *Turning the Soul: Teaching Through Conversation in the High School*, received an American Educational Studies Association Critics Choice Award in 1994. Her *Learning to Teach Through Discussion: The Art of Turning the Soul*, a study of two MSEd students who were learning to lead discussions, was published in 2009. Haroutunian-Gordon is coeditor of special issues of *Teachers College Record* and *Educational Theory* on the topic of listening—an interest that has grown out of her research.

Index